Britain's Future in Europe

"An absolutely invaluable resource for anyone concerned with Britain's evolving relationship with the European Union."

Anthony Giddens
former Director of the London School of Economics,
and member of the House of Lords

"In the finest tradition of British pragmatism: a much needed injection of common sense and seriousness into the British debate on Europe."

François Heisbourg
Fondation pour la Recherche Stratégique, Paris

"This is a comprehensive and cogent analysis of the British government's review of EU competences. While the government was reluctant to draw conclusions from its own review, the CEPS researchers are bolder."

Charles Grant
Director of the Centre for European Reform, London

"This extraordinarily fair-minded and balanced book is a myth-busting exercise of the best kind. Meticulously boiling down every single European policy field to its very essence, the authors (one of Europe's leading think tank teams) are replacing misperception and misrepresentation with sober facts and sound assessments. What they offer is a non-romantic, no-spin, jargon-free, no-hyperbole guidebook to the Brexit debate, highly useful for everyone who wants to navigate this fateful question with a cool head and clear vision."

Jan Techau
Director of Carnegie Europe

The Centre for European Policy Studies (CEPS) is an independent policy research institute in Brussels. Its mission is to produce sound policy research leading to constructive solutions to the challenges facing Europe.

The views expressed in this book are entirely those of the authors and should not be attributed to CEPS or to any other institution with which the authors are associated, or to the European Union, or the government of the United Kingdom.

While this book is based on research conducted by the British government in its Balance of Competences Review, the text indicates when it is citing this source, and when the conclusions are those of the authors.

The authors are most grateful to the Open Society Foundations for their kind support for this project.

Britain's Future in Europe

Reform, renegotiation, repatriation or secession?

Edited by
Michael Emerson

Contributors
Graham Avery
Miroslav Beblavý
Arno Behrens
Steven Blockmans
Hugo Brady
Michael Emerson
Daniel Gros
Alzbeta Hájková
Karel Lannoo
Adam Łazowski
Jorge Núñez Ferrer
Steve Peers
Michael Wriglesworth

Centre for European Policy Studies (CEPS), Brussels
Rowman and Littlefield International, London

Published by Rowman & Littlefield International, Ltd.
Unit A, Whitacre Mews, 26-34 Stannary Street, London SE11 4AB
www.rowmaninternational.com

Rowman & Littlefield International Ltd. is an affiliate of Rowman & Littlefield
4501 Forbes Boulevard, Suite 200, Lanham, Maryland 20706, USA
With additional offices in Boulder, New York, Toronto (Canada), and Plymouth (UK)
www.rowman.com

Centre for European Policy Studies
Place du Congrès 1, B-1000 Brussels
Tel: (32.2) 229.39.11 Fax: (32.2) 219.41.51
E-mail: info@ceps.eu
Website: http://www.ceps.eu

QM LIBRARY
(MILE END)

British Library Cataloguing in Publication Data
A catalogue record for this book is available from the British Library

ISBN: 978-1-78348-372-3

☉™   The paper used in this publication meets the minimum requirements of American National Standard for Information Sciences—Permanence of Paper for Printed Library Materials, ANSI/NISO Z39.48-1992.

Printed in the United States of America

TABLE OF CONTENTS

List of Boxes and Figure

GLOSSARY

BIT	Bilateral Investment Treaty
BSE	Mad cow disease
CAP	Common Agricultural Policy
CBI	Confederation of British Industries
CCCTB	Common Consolidated Corporation Tax Base
CEPS	Centre for European Policy Studies
CfD	Contracts for Difference
CFP	Common Fisheries Policy
CSDP	Common Security and Defence Policy
CFSP	Common Foreign and Security Policy
CJEU	Court of Justice of the European Union
CRD	Capital Requirements Directive
DCFTA	Deep and Comprehensive Free Trade Agreement
DEVCO	Development Cooperation (directorate general of the European Commission)
EBA	European Banking Authority
ECB	European Central Ban
ECHO	European Commission's Humanitarian Aid and Civil Protection department
ECTS	European Credit Transfer and Accumulation System
EEA	European Economic Area
EEAS	European External Action Service
EFTA	European Free Trade Association
EIA	Environmental Impact Assessment
EQF	European Qualifications Framework
ERA	European Research Area
ERDF	European Regional Development Fund
ESA	European Space Agency
ESF	European Social Fund
ESFS	European System of Financial Supervision
ESMA	European Securities Markets Authority
ETS	Emissions Trading System
EURODAC	European Dactyloscopy (fingerprint data base)

EUROSUR	European Border Surveillance System
FDI	Foreign direct investment
FIFA	Federation Internationale Football Association
FP7	7th Framework Programme (of the EU for research)
FTA	Free Trade Agreement
FTT	Financial Transaction Tax
GATS	General Agreement on Trade in Services
GDP	Gross Domestic Product
IPCC	International Panel on Climate Change
IoT	Internet of Things
MERCOSUR	South American Common Market
MRPQ	Mutual Recognition of Professional Qualifications
NATO	North Atlantic Treaty Organization
OMC	Open Method of Coordination
QMV	Qualified Majority Voting
REACH	Registration, Evaluation, Authorisation and Restriction of Chemicals
REFIT	Regulatory Fitness and Performance Programme
SIS	Schengen Information System
SME	Small and medium-sized enterprise
SRM	Single Resolution Mechanism
SSM	Single Supervisory Mechanism
S & P	Subsidiarity and Proportionality
TEU	Treaty of European Union (Lisbon Treaty)
TFEU	Treaty on the Functioning of the European Union (Lisbon Treaty)
TRIPS	Agreement on Trade-Related Aspects of Intellectual Property Rights
TTIP	Transatlantic Trade and Investment Partnership
UEFA	Union of European Football Associations
UKIP	United Kingdom Independence Party
UNFCCC	United Nations Framework Convention on Climate Change
VAT	Value Added Tax
VIS	Visa Information System
WTO	World Trade Organisation

About the Authors

Michael Emerson, Associate Senior Research Fellow, Centre for European Policy Studies (CEPS)

Graham Avery, Senior Member of St. Antony's College, Oxford University

Arno Behrens, Research Fellow, Centre for European Policy Studies (CEPS)

Miroslav Beblavý, Senior Research Fellow, Centre for European Policy Studies (CEPS) and Member of Parliament in Slovakia

Steven Blockmans, Senior Research Fellow, Head of EU Foreign Policy, Centre for European Policy Studies (CEPS), and Professor of EU External Relations Law and Governance, University of Amsterdam

Hugo Brady, Visiting Fellow, London School of Economics

Daniel Gros, Director, Centre for European Policy Studies (CEPS)

Alzbeta Hájková, Assistant to Miroslav Beblavý at the Slovakian parliament

Karel Lannoo, Chief Executive Officer, Centre for European Policy Studies (CEPS)

Adam Łazowski, Professor of EU Law, University of Westminster

Jorge Núñez Ferrer, Senior Research Fellow, Centre for European Policy Studies (CEPS)

Steven Peers, Professor of Law, Essex University

Michael Wriglesworth, Senior Research Fellow, Centre for European Policy Studies (CEPS)

PREFACE

"What we need in Britain is a renegotiation of our relationship with the EU and then a referendum where the British people decide do we stay in this reformed organisation or do we leave it?"
David Cameron, 20 October 2014

This book is rather unusual. It is about the conclusions that the British government chose *not* to draw from its own in-depth and impressive research into the workings of the EU.

The reasons why it chose not to draw conclusions are understandable. The coalition parties differ radically in their positions on Europe. They could agree to undertake a comprehensive review of the actual policies of the EU, based on evidence to be collected openly from independent sources, without prejudicing the conclusions to be drawn. The advantage for the general public is that the basis has been provided for the shaping of informed opinion.

The main point of this study is to aid those who are thinking about the possible referendum on Europe, which the British Prime Minister David Cameron promises to hold in 2017, or maybe earlier, if the Conservative Party wins an outright majority in the next general election. Our ambition was to distil a huge amount of information (3,000 pages of evidence) down to manageable proportions. We do this in several stages. The primary sources are the British government's 32 Reviews, all accessible with online references (Appendix A). The main body of this book condenses each of these Reviews to just a few pages, while adding our own assessments, which are pulled together in the concluding chapter and summarised very briefly in the Executive Summary. Those who may be unconvinced by our assessments can retrace the arguments back to the full original sources. We have included a section on the hypothesis of secession, which was not discussed in any depth in the Reviews.

Given the reliance here on research published by the British government, we have to be clear to whom the conclusions drawn in this book can be attributed. Our work has been completely independent of the British government, although we have had technical contacts with the officials concerned.

While the motivation for this book has been the 'British question', its content is relevant for those in other member states and the EU institutions themselves who wrestle with the challenges of contemporary Europe. Britain's policies on Europe are controversial, but the UK government has actually done the rest of Europe a considerable service through this project.

I am most grateful to colleagues, at CEPS and elsewhere, for contributing their specialised knowledge of the themes they have treated. In particular, Steven Blockmans contributed on foreign policy and several other topics, Graham Avery on agriculture and fisheries, Miroslav Beblavý and Alzbeta Hájková on social and employment policies, Arno Behrens on energy, Hugo Brady on immigration, Daniel Gros on the economic and monetary union, Karel Lannoo on financial markets, Adam Łazowski on secession, Jorge Núñez Ferrer on cohesion, Steve Peers on civil justice, and Michael Wriglesworth on environment. For the rest the editor is responsible.

We also thank Jackie West and Anne Harrington at CEPS, and Alison Howson at Rowman & Littlefield International, for their valuable editorial assistance.

Finally, we are greatly indebted to the Open Society Foundations for supporting the project.

Michael Emerson
Brussels, February 2015

EXECUTIVE SUMMARY
COMMON SENSE AND NOBLE IDEAS

The British government has assembled the most comprehensive-ever assessment of the workings of the European Union, called the 'Balance of Competences Review'. This is based on 32 volumes and 3,000 pages of evidence submitted by over 1,500 independent sources, now published in coherent analyses.

The terms of reference for this research were that policy conclusions should not be drawn in these published documents, but be left to the readers. This is an invitation that we are happy to take up.

The central question in the Review is whether the competences (i.e. legal powers and responsibilities) of the European Union are excessive or not. In no case does the evidence support the repatriation of a competence at the level at which they are defined in the Lisbon Treaty.

Most of these competences are shared with member states, which means that the detailed balances are open to adjustment over time and in the light of experience in either centralising or decentralising directions.

The evidence shows that the sharing of competences between the EU and member states has mostly been refined through years of negotiation and experience of reaching plausible balances.

The argument that the European Union is 'unreformable' is shown to be simplistic and untrue.

On the contrary, the reform and policy improvement agenda – past, present and future – covers almost every policy domain.

The EU now gives increasing priority to weeding out unnecessary 'red tape', with a new top-level appointment at the

European Commission to oversee this, which corresponds to a key British demand.

The amount of EU-based legislation adopted by national parliaments needs an objective perspective. A thorough House of Common study showed that for the UK 6.8% of primary legislation and 14.1 % of secondary legislation had a role in implementing EU law, compared to various political speeches alleging as much as 75% without quoting any serious source.

The UK attaches the highest priority to the single market, and has since the 1980s played, and continues to play, a major role in shaping its reform. As a result the number of EU laws passed each year saw a high peak in the 1980s and early 1990s when the single market was being completed with strong British support. However these numbers have declined by two-thirds since then.

The UK works as promoter of more effective and enhanced (not diluted) EU policies in key single market sectors where there is important work in progress. These include, notably:

- the single market for services, across the board
- financial markets
- energy and climate change
- the digital sector.

Two much criticised sectors have undergone major reform:

- fisheries, with key reforms in 2013
- agriculture.

In the case of agriculture, reforms in the 1990s saw a radical shift from production support to decoupled income support (ending 'butter mountains', etc.), and leading on to a continuing decline in its share of the EU budget.

There are two other areas where the UK has been successful in advancing key interests, namely:

- higher education with the Erasmus+ programme;
- winning a large share of EU research grants .

The UK has already negotiated or re-negotiated huge opt-outs or special arrangements for those EU policies that it does not want for itself. These include, notably:

- Opt-out of the eurozone, not only of the euro currency, but also from coercive elements in broader macroeconomic and fiscal policy coordination procedures. The UK thus stands aside from the hugely important ongoing issues of systemic reform and macroeconomic regulation of the eurozone.

- Opt-out of the Schengen area, thus retaining control of its own borders.
- Opt-out of the domain of justice and home affairs, except for the possibility to pick and choose what elements it wants to opt back into.
- In the past it has opted out and then back in to various social policies.
- A special rebate on budgetary contributions, compensating for low farm-subsidy receipts.

The UK currently seeks to curb immigration from the rest of the EU, and there are moderate ways of doing this that do not contradict the freedom of movement of labour, and where the UK can find allies.

In specific policy areas where the UK is concerned not to see erosion of its sovereign national powers, there are unanimity safeguards to prevent this. These include, notably:

- foreign and security policy
- taxation.

There is no hypothetical scenario for secession spelt out in the Reviews, nor is it set out in operational terms by any political party. However, our own observations are as follows:

- The legal procedures for secession exist. But if it was decided to pick and choose what to repeal from the mass of UK legislation implementing EU single market law, and negotiate a new relationship with the EU, the process would be complex and hazardous, with risks of legal uncertainty in the meantime.
- The only sound economic scenario to avoid these risks and the loss of guaranteed access to the single market would be to join the European Economic Area), i.e. to stick to single market law.
- But this would mean a serious loss of sovereignty compared to the status quo, defeating the presumed political purpose of secession.

- The overwhelming majority of business leaders warn against secession.

- The UK would become a marginal actor in Europe and lose status on the world stage. The Review sees the EU as a 'multiplier' of UK interests; secession would be a categorical 'de-multiplier' of these interests.

At the level of fundamental values, the European Union has achieved peace, democracy and respect for human rights in a large and growing part of the continent of Europe. The UK's secession would weaken this transformative achievement, which in wider Europe cannot be taken for granted (Russia's aggression in Ukraine is a reminder of this).

The UK's threat to withdraw from the European Convention on Human Rights and the European Court of Human Rights in Strasbourg, while not directly a matter for the EU, would also undermine the cause of human rights in wider Europe.

Overall, the evidence supports a common-sense view that British interests are best served by continuing membership of the European Union, combined with pushing ahead with reform processes, while retaining its important opt-outs. The essential point is that this conclusion is not a government or party-political statement; it is based on the evidence of a comprehensive collection of voluntary submissions by well-informed and independent stakeholders.

Part I - Questions

1. What is the Balance of Competences Review?

The ultimate question is whether Britain should stay in the EU or secede, which Prime Minister Cameron has committed to put to a binding referendum in 2017, in the event that the Conservative Party wins outright in the general election of May 2015.

The referendum is intended to resolve this question once and for all, while setting a target date sufficiently far ahead to allow for negotiations with the EU and other member states to solve as many of the perceived problems as possible in the meantime, and for public debate to mature in parallel.

To prepare the ground for defining its policy on Europe, in July 2012 the government launched a "Review of the Balance of Competences" of the EU, namely the balance between the EU and the member states in the distribution of powers. This is described in official documents as "an audit of what the EU does and how it affects the UK."[1]

The core question that the Balance of Competence Review addresses is whether the distribution of competences between the EU and national levels is about right or is in need of change, which could mean changes in either direction, with repatriation of competences from the EU back to the national level, or the strengthening of competences at the EU level, or both at the same time. These changes might represent mere adjustments or be more radical in amplitude.

From the outset the Review was intended to collect objective evidence, with open invitations to any interested organisations, companies or persons to make submissions that would be

---

[1] See Appendix A for website links to the individual Reviews, and the page numbers in the text refer to these sources.

analysed by the civil servants of the relevant government departments and published with transparent attribution of sources. In all, 32 sectoral reviews were commissioned, covering the entire landscape of EU policies, and the results have now been published, totalling around 3,000 pages of evidence submitted by some 1,500 independent individuals or organisations (see Annex A for links to the published materials).

As to the rules of the game, the terms of reference for these reviews were not to reach explicit conclusions and recommendations, but rather to provide objective materials for others to do so. In fact, the many volumes of evidence provide a unique resource for anyone seriously interested in this question. Nothing like this has been done before – and there are many textbooks on European affairs. For this reason the present authors wished to distil conclusions from this substantial basis, reducing the mass of evidence to a short book while subjecting the findings to our own independent assessments.

Regarding the political context, the Prime Minister set out his terms of engagement in the European question in his 'Bloomberg' speech in January 2013.[2] While important as a political statement, the speech gave little indication of what he wanted, beyond such expressions as "the EU must change", "power must be able to flow back to member states, not just away from them", and the need "to negotiate a new settlement with our European partners" and for the EU to be "more flexible, more adaptable and more open". A year later, in March 2014, the Prime Minister reiterated his position, using much the same language of negotiating a "new settlement", with emphasis on "no to ever-closer union"; "no to unnecessary interference and red tape"; and more specific reference to immigration and "the free movement to take up work, not free benefits".[3] Many Conservative MPs talk of the need to "repatriate" competences of the EU, but mostly

---

[2] David Cameron, speech at Bloomberg on the Future of Europe, 23 January 2013 (https://www.gov.uk/government/speeches/eu-speech-at-bloomberg).

[3] David Cameron, "The EU is not working and we will change it", *Daily Telegraph*, 17 March 2014.

without stating which competences they have in mind, beyond the frequent references to immigration and certain labour market rules.

Overall, there is a huge contrast between the comprehensive and concrete survey approach of the Balance of Competence Review on the one hand, and political speeches that are generally thin in terms of operational content on the other. It is the task of the former to inform the latter.

2.   What are the EU's competences?

The EU has accumulated many competences in recent decades. These are codified in several categories in the Lisbon Treaty, signed in December 2007.[4]

The EU has a few *'exclusive'* competences, where only the EU has the power to legislate in these areas. These are mainly in the field of international trade, and monetary policy in the eurozone. In these cases, the exclusivity is driven by practical realities, since customs union or monetary union could not function alongside multiple national policies.

The EU has a greater number of *'shared'* competences, where both the EU and member states can legislate, with rules to prevent conflicting laws. The respective shares of the EU and member states can change over time, in either direction, depending on the extent of new legislation at either level, or the repeal of existing laws. Many of these competences are in the broad area of the single market, which requires many technical regulations to govern the supply of goods and services.

The EU has several *'supporting'* competences, where it may carry out certain actions to support, coordinate or supplement the actions of member states, but where the main responsibility lies with the member states, such as for public health and education.

---

[4] More precisely, in Title I of the Treaty on the Functioning of the European Union – TFEU.

Box 1. *The competences of the European Union as defined in the Lisbon Treaty*

Exclusive competences

- Customs union competition policy
- International trade policy
- Monetary policy for members of the eurozone
- Some aspects of fisheries policy

Shared competences

- Internal market
- Social policy
- Cohesion (regional) policy
- Agriculture and fisheries
- Environment
- Consumer protection
- Transport
- Energy
- Freedom, security and justice
- Aspects of public health
- Research and technological development[5]
- Development cooperation and humanitarian assistance[6]

Supporting competences

- Protection of human health
- Industry
- Culture
- Tourism
- Education, training, youth and sport
- Civil protection

Two of the most important fields are the subject of more specific description under the Lisbon Treaty. For *economic policy,* for example, the treaty states that "member states shall coordinate their economic and employment policies within arrangements

---

[5] This sector has a modified form of shared competence, with the member states free to implement their own policies in these areas.

[6] This sector has a similar modified form of shared competence.

provided by the Treaty, which the Union shall have competence to provide" (Article 2.3, TFEU). These 'arrangements' include a considerable amount of legislation, most importantly for the eurozone.

For *foreign policy* the treaty says that "The Union shall have competence, in accordance with the provisions of the Treaty on European Union, to define and implement a common foreign and security policy), including the framing of a common defence policy" (Article 2.2, TFEU). The method remains largely inter-governmental here, however, with unanimity among member states forming the basic decision-making rule.

The core method of the official Balance of Competence Review has been to work systematically through all of these competences, obtaining independent evidence on how each has been functioning. This has been a huge undertaking, never before conducted on this scale. For each of these Reviews the bottom-line question is whether the competence of the EU in this area, relative to the powers of the member states, is about right. Or are the EU's competences excessive, or insufficient, for effective policy-making?

The main part of the present study consists of summary assessments by expert authors in each area of the findings and judgments made in the 32 Reviews.

The Reviews go deeper than the core question of whether the EU's competences are 'about right' or not, and consider where there is scope for improving efficiency and effectiveness in the functioning of present competences, without necessarily calling into question their attribution to the EU. This is material for the 'reform' agenda.

3.   What are the underlying issues?

While the question of whether or not to secede from the EU is, in principle, clear, the answers should be based on the clarification of a second tier of questions that go into the underlying issues at stake. These concern both the conditions for continued membership and the conditions for secession.

On the conditions for continued membership, the political debate in the UK is using three keywords: reform, renegotiation and repatriation. There are crucial differences between these eventualities.

Reform is a loose and maybe over-used term. It can embrace any steps that improve the status quo, either at the level of individual policies and laws, or on a grander scale. In the context of the EU, reform means measures taken by the EU as a whole, without special provision for a single member state, such as the UK. The political speeches of the British government mostly refer to achieving a "reformed EU", which would be the basis for the government to recommend a Yes vote at the proposed referendum. UK opinion polls are clear on this point: there is a large majority in favour of staying in a "reformed EU", whereas the majority in favour of remaining in the EU without any such qualification is slender, or questionable. Reform is also part of the vocabulary of other EU leaders, and so in principle points to a positive way ahead. But then comes the question: What reforms? Here the Balance of Competence Review helps identify at the operational level where EU policies could be made more efficient, where so-called 'red tape' could be cut, etc.

Renegotiation is about the UK receiving special treatment or 'opt-outs' in relation to EU laws and policies. This has been done in the past, notably for contributions to the EU budget. As regards opt-outs, the major cases of the euro and Schengen area were negotiated at a time when these policies were being shaped. The practical question is whether further opt-outs might be sought by the UK and successfully negotiated with other member states.

Repatriation is about returning competences to the member states. This leads to the question of which competences might be targets for repatriation, and at what level. The first level consists of competences as defined in the Lisbon Treaty (as listed above). Repatriation would require unanimous agreement on treaty changes, followed by repeal of the numerous operational laws of the EU that have been passed on the basis of the treaty provisions. The second level consists of the individual legal regulations and directives, which can be repealed on an individual basis without withdrawing the EU competence at the treaty level. This enters into the detail of EU policies, and especially the many 'shared' competences of the EU, where the relative proportions of the sharing can be adjusted.

On the *conditions for secession*, the British government would first need to work out what it would seek. The idea of a simple, big-bang, unilateral repeal of all EU law on the British statute book is not plausible, since it would create a huge legal void and economic uncertainty. There would have to be a negotiated settlement. A number of scenarios are discussed in Part III, and each of these leads to the question of what the political and economic consequences for the UK would be.

PART II - EVIDENCE

1. Core single market policies

1.1 *Single market overview*

The Review of the single market surveys a vast field, with many of the subsequent Reviews going into more detail sector by sector. Overall, this Review observes a broad consensus that the single market is the EU's core mechanism for advancing and sustaining its high level of economic development.

It highlights the strong influence of the UK on the development of the single market. The big move towards completing the single market began in 1985, when the objective was set to achieve this goal by 1992 with the aid of 279 legislative measures, masterminded by Commissioner Lord Cockfield. There were two general keys to this achievement: first the move to qualified majority voting in the Council, and second the increased emphasis on the method of mutual recognition as opposed to harmonisation.

Business interests note that the single market regime brings legal certainty and market openness, but also regulatory burdens. But these burdens are not necessarily greater than national regulations, and of course enterprises engaged in cross-border business are saved from having to master 28 different regulatory regimes.

In seeking to summarise what powers remain in the hands of member states the Review rightly comments that there is no clear boundary between EU and national competences, but rather a continuous process of interactions. Member states remain free to act as long as they do not infringe upon EU law, and in particular any restrictions on the free movement of goods, services, people and capital are subject to legal challenge.

The Review analyses effects on the economy, on economic actors, and on policy-making.

In goods markets integration in the single market has meant the development of complex cross-border supply chains for both material and service inputs. Integration has lagged behind in some important network industries, however, including energy, telecoms, transport and the digital IT sector. Whereas the early single market agenda has now reached a stage of maturity, for the network industries much remains to be done, and many popular comments that the EU is 'over-regulated' miss this point.

As regards foreign direct investment (FDI), there is a particular British interest in the single market, since the UK has been winning a disproportionate share of the EU total, notably from Japan. It is generally thought that international investors would downgrade the ranking of the UK as an investment location in the event of secession from the EU and its loss of completely secure access to the single market.

Regarding the regulatory burden on businesses, there is a broad distinction in the Review between large internationally oriented businesses that place a high value on legal certainty for their operations, and small- and medium-sized businesses that do not export and would prefer less regulation. UK respondents have two particular concerns; that the UK itself may be 'gold-plating' its implementation of EU regulations with unnecessarily costly provisions (but the evidence for this is not clear-cut); and that other member states may be less diligent than the UK in implementing such measures.

As regards the policy-making process, the Review notes the significant influence of the UK in pushing single market policy in a liberalising direction, and indeed other liberally oriented member states are concerned that secession by the UK would weaken this strategic orientation. For UK interests contemplating the prospect of secession there would be a double risk; both that access to the EU market would become uncertain, and that the single market al ime itself could become less liberal.

Looking to the future, the Review considers that a new long-term strategy for the single market will anyway be called for after the renewal of the Commission and Parliament in 2014. On the one hand this will need to fit in with the growing globalisation of the world economy, and on the other hand to be reconciled with the widening scope of eurozone economic governance, notably in financial markets. On the question of specific priorities the Review highlights the case for the 'digital single market'.

Finally, the Review asks where the UK might gain from the EU doing less in the single market area. If this were to mean weakening the depth of integration, "it is hard to see that could be in the UK's interest" (p.57 of the Review). Although it is easy to say that the EU should regulate less, justifying this in operational terms and deciding on what and how to regulate less is more of a challenge. The Review acknowledges the continuous pressure from markets and technological change to develop new or to revise existing regulations.

"The EU could help itself in this area by, for example, ensuring it has a properly functioning mechanism that screened legislative proposals more systematically and objectively, for example that a proposal would only proceed if it clearly had a positive impact on growth" (p.57).

The Commission's REFIT programme aims to achieve this, which the Review does not mention.[7]

Assessment

At the strategic level the Review shows the UK to have been a driver in support of a liberal regulatory order in the single market. The appreciable economic benefits of the single market to the EU as a whole including the UK are considered matters of broad consensus. The UK's interest in the single market is highlighted by its success in attracting a disproportionate share of foreign direct investment from third countries, which would be undermined by secession.

The Review does not explicitly discuss the consequences of hypothetical secession for the UK's access to the single market A seceding UK would surely wish to retain secure access to the EU single market, but the only evident model for doing this is the EEA regime enjoyed by Norway, which the British Prime Minister has ruled out on the grounds that it would mean an unacceptable loss

---

[7] European Commission, "Regulatory Fitness and Performance (REFIT): Results and Next Steps", COM(2013)685, final, 2 October 2013.

of sovereignty. Yet anything less than this opens up a huge unknown as to what the post-secession regime would consist of. One hypothesis is that existing EU market legislation would remain in force unless and until it were repealed or replaced. If the UK were to adopt a selective approach its present guarantee of full access to the single market would be undermined. What is certain is that a seceding UK would have no say in new EU regulations or the revision of old ones, and no assurance at all that the direction of EU single market policies would be in the UK's interests. As the Review clearly shows, the EU's single market regulatory processes are in continuous interaction with the dynamics of globalisation and technological change, so merely keeping existing EU regulation on the books would soon become an obsolete option.

Postscript. Regarding the 'red tape' issue, and subsequent to publication of the Review, the Juncker Commission taking office in October 2014 appointed Frans Timmermans to the new position of First Vice-President, charged with the task of screening legislative proposals for subsidiarity and proportionality (discussed in more detail in section 7.2, below).

The evidence at a glance – single market overview

Strategic priority for the UK, with leadership role since the '1992' programme reform

Large majority support for EU competence

Advantages of legal certainty, openness, and avoidance of 28 different regulatory regimes

National regulations would not necessarily be lighter, some 'gold-plating' by UK

1.2   Free movement of goods

This Review covers much the same ground as the preceding one at the level of general strategic arguments, confirming the priority given to the single market by successive British governments. It does go into more detail on Lord Cockfield's programme to eliminate cross-border restrictions by 1992, however. The plan had two key innovations that overcame previous obstacles that slowed progress towards the single market objective to a snail's pace. The first was to switch the decision-making rule for single market legislation to qualified majority rather than unanimity, which enabled the Cockfield plan to be implemented. The second was to reduce the burden of harmonisation of product standards by a 'new approach' extending the use of the mutual recognition principle. From 1979 onwards there had been a number of rulings by the European Court of Justice that established the mutual recognition principle, for example in a number of landmark cases for liqueurs and beer.[8]

The Review explains in some detail how the new approach of the '1992 programme' overhauled the previous system more generally and radically. Legislation would be restricted to identifying the essential health or safety requirements, and technical specifications were now to be entrusted to European standardisation bodies. If products were made to conform to these standards they would gain the 'presumption of conformity'. Manufacturers could still produce goods according to other technical standards, but in this case they could be required to justify them to the mutual recognition authorities of member states. The new approach is now taken for granted, such that reversal to the situation that prevailed some 30 years ago would be unthinkable. Still, it may be noted that Prime Minister Cameron's flagship speech on Europe on 23 January 2013 barely recognised this, with wording such as "the EU cannot harmonise everything".

However, the conclusions of the review on the EU's competences for the free movement of goods may be considered to reflect the broad European consensus on the question, not just a

---

[8] The landmark *Cassis de Dijon* ruling of 1979 where Germany blocked the import of this French liqueur on the grounds that its alcohol content was below the minimum set by German law, even though the product was in conformity with French law. The Court of Justice ruled that an importing member state could not forbid the sale of a product that was in conformity with the exporting member state. It took time for this principle to gain general acceptance, however, as was seen in the 1988 case around the German beer 'purity' law (*Reinheitsgebot*) dating back to 1487, which was being used to prevent the import of Dutch *Heineken* beer, for example, on the grounds that it endangered the health of German consumers. The Court of Justice again supported the case that these imports could not be blocked.

British view. "The majority of respondents to this review, including most respondent from business organisations and individual firms, supported the current balance of competence on the free movement of goods.... They felt that the advantages of EU action – for example a level playing field for UK businesses and a single transparent set of rules with scope for legal redress – outweighed the costs arising from administrative burdens, regulatory costs or policy trade-offs" (p.6).

Beyond this general assessment, the Review goes in some detail into a number of key issues.

Supply chain economics are seen to have become an increasingly important factor in the structure and functioning of European industry. The UK's automotive sector sources 90% of motor vehicle components from the EU, for example. For this and other sectors the need for fast, reliable and low-cost shipment of goods across borders for 'just-in-time' delivery is a competitivity factor of paramount importance. The removal of the need to make customs declarations has represented a major administrative simplification and cost-reducing factor. This is taken for granted now, but would re-emerge as an issue if the UK left the customs union.

The EU's competence in the field of intellectual property rights is a complex matter, which the Review examines. The findings from stakeholder representations were that the EU's responsibilities for the 'Trade Mark' and 'Design Right' received strong support. The European Patents Convention and Patent Office have simplified the process of obtaining patent protection across Europe, while the forthcoming Unitary Patent and Unified Patent Court are seen as strengthening enforcement.

There remain some exceptional categories where member states can restrict imports of goods from elsewhere in the EU. UK legislation, in particular, can require import or export licenses for antiquities of cultural value, drugs, firearms, animals and military goods. Customs controls are governed by EU law but execution remains in the hands of national customs services, and criminal offences are dealt with under national legislation.

The Review reports findings on the costs of EU regulations as well as the benefits of open markets. Small businesses, especially those that do not export or import, complain most about the burden of EU regulations. However, the counterfactual case of not being subject to EU regulations would not mean freedom from regulation. UK manufacturers would need to comply with EU standards in any case if they wished to export to the EU, and the UK would itself probably adopt laws and procedures similar to those set by the EU. At the same time it is considered desirable to devise regulatory regimes that where possible mitigate burdens on small enterprises, and this is an issue that the Commission seeks to address in a number of areas.

The Review reports concern by representative business organisations over unequal performance of member states in implementing and enforcing EU rules. In the British case, while there is widespread demand for a light regulatory touch, there is also a legal culture that favours strict enforcement.

Assessment

The majority of evidence presented suggests that the balance of competence for the free movement of goods and intellectual property rights was in the UK's interest. While some respondents advocated withdrawing competence from the EU, most respondents felt it better to work with and through the EU institutions. While there is concern for the EU's competences to be executed more efficiently and effectively, the case for drastic deregulation found little support. Outside the EU, the UK would find itself adopting much the same regulatory standards, but with the disadvantage that divergences in product standards would reduce economies of scale on production lines, and lead to increased costs and prices. However, even inside the EU, product standards are voluntary rather than mandatory, such that if enterprises wished to aim predominantly at external markets there is nothing in the regulatory regime preventing them from producing goods according to the client country's standards.

The evidence at a glance – free movement of goods
Key '1992' reform: mutual recognition for goods standards
Less reliance on harmonisation
Trans-European supply-chain economics needs EU competence
Useful complementary competences for Trade Marks and Patents

> *Little support for return to national regulations that would re-open the field for unfair practices between member states*

1.3 Free movement of services

This is one of the most important chapters in the Balance of Competences Review, for several reasons. Services account for an increasing share of the modern economy and involve a highly complex and differentiated set of sub-sectors, with correspondingly complex regulatory requirements. The British government is at the forefront of those pushing for 'completion' of the internal market for services, which is currently still fragmented by a huge variety of inconsistent national regulations. There are also technological trends in the economy that blur the distinction between goods, where the internal market is largely completed, versus services, where it is less so.

The Review recounts the evolution of the EU's competence in this field. The free movement of services and freedom of establishment for individuals and companies was already enshrined in the Treaty of Rome and carried over in successive treaties up to the current Treaty of Lisbon. Individuals and companies can go to the European Court of Justice to secure enforcement of their rights under the treaties, and as a result a wide body of case law has developed. From the early days this put much emphasis on the prohibition of discrimination on grounds of nationality. However, this approach has been progressively extended to measures that, while not strictly discriminatory, would be liable to impede the supply of services from other member states.

Nonetheless, many remaining restrictions meant that the services sector still lagged some way behind the goods sector in the degree of true openness in the single market, and given the growing importance of services to the economy it was increasingly felt that a more ambitious approach was required. This led to the proposed Services Directive of 2004, which sought to radically apply the 'country of origin' principle, or in other words mutual recognition of the regulatory regimes of each member state. This went beyond what the political market could take, however, and political polemics emerged, as famously represented by the 'Polish plumber' who would be undercutting the native plumber in France.

As a result a highly complex directive finally emerged in 2006, with many sub-sectors securing protection for a host of specific national provisions. The directive is nevertheless recognised as having made a major advance in opening services markets. It applies to a very wide range of services that, in spite of various exclusions, are estimated to account for 46% of the EU's GDP. The directive is described as being 'horizontal' since it sets out general principles to be observed for all service sectors that have not been explicitly excluded. The included sectors cover the regulated professions, craftsmen, business-related services, distributive trades, tourism, leisure services, construction services, information services, rental and leasing services, hotels and restaurants, real estate services etc. The excluded services are in several cases regulated separately by the EU under sector-specific legislation (financial services, transport, telecommunications, etc.), and the main real exclusions from EU competences are public health, public education and social services.

The main substance of the directive consists of two lists, first of "prohibitions", and secondly of "requirements to be evaluated" for the service sectors covered. The prohibitions include discrimination on grounds of nationality and many detailed restrictions on the activities of companies or service providers (e.g. a company cannot be required to make its main place of business in the member state where it supplies a service, or cannot be required to pre-register, or to limit its service for a certain length of time). The requirements to be evaluated, to assure that they are not restricting the openness of the single market, cover such cases as where the service provider should have a certain number of employees, or be restricted to one location, or have certain types of shareholders.

Because of the huge complexity of the task of policing what practices might be inconsistent with the directive, there is recourse to a 'mutual evaluation' process of peer review of each member state's practice by other member states. Member states are also required to undertake 'screening' exercises to test the compliance of their practices with the EU legislation. This has led to the elimination of thousands of illegitimate restrictions and, in the view of a detailed CEPS) report, the removal of barriers on a scale "far more extensive and rigorous than could reasonably have been expected".[9]

For professions the EU has developed legislation for the Mutual Recognition of Professional Qualifications (MRPQ). This legislation has recently been revised with important new features, notably a transparency process to subject national practices to peer pressure and possible challenge, and the introduction of the European Professional Card, which may be adopted profession-by-profession.

The digital single market receives particular attention in the Review, and this is an example of an area where the British government recognises the need for an important application and development of EU competences, and has established a list of six priorities for this sector. All of these rely on regulatory action by the EU covering copyright, data protection, payment services, high-speed broadband, telecoms and e-commerce. The digital economy is the fastest growing sub-sector of manifest importance for the EU's competitivity, and for this sector EU regulation is inescapable, as is the need for Europe to take a solid common position in negotiations with the United States in this area.

In the area of public procurement the EU has adopted a package of new rules, which contributors of evidence to the report generally consider to be valuable in improving public procurement in the UK itself as well as in opening other markets. The defence procurement sector is dealt with separately, however, and is subject to efforts by the Commission to extend its effective EU competence. While the case for rationalisation of European defence industries is widely recognised, various stakeholders treat the prospect of enhanced EU competence cautiously, in view of its implications for national security.

---

[9] Federica Mustilli and Jacques Pelkmans, "Access Barriers to Service Markets – Mapping, tracing, understanding and measuring", CEPS Special Report No. 77, CEPS, Brussels, June 2013.

Assessment

There was general support for the current balance of competence in this broad area, with the advantages of EU action outweighing the disadvantages. There were also calls for greater integration of the single market for services, and the completion of the digital single market was cited as an example. It was recognised that even non-exporting businesses have benefited from the liberalisation of domestic service markets, and that any national legislation would not be dissimilar to the current EU regime.

Services are more important to the UK economy than for many other member states, and business associations welcome liberalisation at the EU level for this reason. The British Chambers of Commerce note that "free movement of services is a critical aspect of EU membership as it provides our members with access to a market of 500 million people. The UK is the second largest exporter of services in the world". The Federation of Small Businesses notes that those of its members that do service business abroad do so overwhelmingly with other European countries.

Incomplete or ineffective implementation of existing services legislation has hindered the development of the free movement of services. There is scope to go further in services liberalisation within the current level of EU competence, extending the 'country of origin' principle further within specific sub-sectors.

There has to be consistency in the narrative calling for completion of the internal market for services and a reduction of regulations coming out of Brussels. Popular calls for cutting EU 'red tape' are often too general and simplistic, failing to recognise that if the UK's national interest in the completion of the services market is to be achieved, many inconsistent national regulations will have to be replaced by European legislation.

The evidence at a glance – services
Broad support for EU competence, strong UK economic interests
UK highly active on the reform agenda to complete internal market
EU regulation needed to replace inconsistent national regulations
Digital sector urgently needs more developed EU policy

1.4 Free movement of capital and financial services[*]

This is one of the most detailed and complex case studies in the entire Balance of Competence Review, with a very substantial documentation of evidence. This is not surprising, given that financial services are vital for the City and the UK economy in general. The City is the second largest global financial centre, and a leader in many sectors. For a large and diverse financial hub like London, free branching and free provision of services across the whole of the EU are considerable benefits, and any other regime would be a considerable disadvantage for the City. However, the overarching need to find solutions to the financial crisis that began in 2007 brings huge complexities to the interactions between EU financial markets policies and those of the eurozone.

The EU's regulatory regime, as with international rules and standards in the financial markets sector, has been subject to dramatic reform since the onset of the financial crisis in 2007. While the EU's policies before the crisis focused on opening up the EU internal market, since the crisis the emphasis has shifted massively onto the issues of financial stability and the soundness of banks.

In response to the global financial crisis, reforms at the EU level were initiated in 2009 with the recommendations of the de Larosière report,[10] which noted the grave shortcomings of the existing system of fragmented national supervisory authorities. Enhanced EU competence in this field became a strategic imperative for the EU economy as a whole and the UK in particular. The Review records how the de Larosière report led eventually to the establishment of a completely new European System of Financial Supervision (ESFS), with several agencies created in 2011, including the European Banking Authority (EBA) located in London, and the European Securities and Markets Authority (ESMA) located in Paris.

---

[*] Section contributed by Karel Lannoo.

[10] Report of "The High Level Group on Financial Supervision in the EU", chaired by Jacques de Larosière, 25 February 2009 (http://ec.europa.eu/internal_market/finances/docs/de_larosiere_report_en.pdf).

The EBA is entrusted with devising the European Single Rulebook, which had been proposed by the UK government in 2009 before its subsequent adoption by the European Council. The Single Rulebook aims to provide a set of harmonised rules that financial institutions throughout the EU must respect. It allows the EU to adopt more directly applicable regulations and implementing rules. The disadvantage of such a rulebook may be a lack of proportionality, which is certainly an issue for less developed financial centres and systems. But it should be noted that the UK was at the forefront of advocating the Single Rulebook in order to protect the integrity of EU wholesale financial markets, which are at the heart of the City's interests.

Going beyond these developments in the EU-wide system, eurozone member states have been driven to take more radical steps to defend their financial system. Under the heading 'banking union', these initiatives comprise a Single Supervisory Mechanism (SSM) run by the European Central Bank, and a Single Resolution Mechanism (SRM) to handle emergency cases of failing banks. The UK has negotiated for itself (and any other non-euro member state) provisions for it not to participate in the banking union, and at the same time to protect its interests against possible discriminatory measures taken by the eurozone. These protections concern the role of the EBA in relation to the Single Resolution Mechanism, and the EBA's relations with the European Central Bank as bank supervisor. The detail of these provisions is about avoiding discrimination, sticking to common EU competition policy rules and voting practice in the EBA (p.18). Given the volume of interactions between the functioning of EU financial markets and that of the eurozone, the key point to note here for the UK is that with good will on both sides it proved possible to successfully negotiate both non-participation in the banking union and non-discrimination against the non-participating member states.

The Review still argues that significant reform of the EU's policy-making framework is needed, and that the quality of policy-making is uneven. These criticisms are no different from what is heard in other financial centres or from other players in the EU. It should be recalled that many problems with policy-making originate from the wishes of UK policy-makers, such as for the

Single Rulebook, or are a reaction to some controversial practices in the UK financial market, notably bonuses (on which more below).

Many of the respondents made detailed and targeted criticisms, covering "the quality of the Commission's impact assessments, consultations, and policy-making and policy proposals". However "respondents had few criticisms to make where the Commission had consulted properly or faithfully transposed international standards" (p.86). These reactions can be heard in other countries as well, or in other sectors. It is widely acknowledged that re-regulation of the financial sector had to be pushed through at lightning speed after the financial crisis, and was largely agreed at global level, in the context of the London and subsequent G-20 Summits. The EU Commission could have reacted faster, but expertise was probably lacking more within the European Parliament and many member states in the EU Council. The quality of impact assessments can certainly be improved upon, but interest groups often have very biased definitions of impact assessments.

The Review refers extensively to the three cases in which the UK challenged EU law before the European Court of Justice (CJEU). The first concerns the Short Selling Regulation, and the possibility for the European Securities and Markets Authority (ESMA) to ban short selling in emergency situations, which the UK challenged on the grounds that the powers conferred to ESMA were unlawful. This challenge was dismissed by the Court on all grounds. The CJEU found that in an emergency situation such measures taken by ESMA would be in the interests of guarding financial stability. The review cites the Bar Council's response to the Court judgment, arguing that its reasoning was "very troubling".

The second case challenged, but has not yet settled, concerns about access to euro-denominated financial instruments outside the eurozone, which the UK challenges on single market grounds. The location policy of the ECB specifies that clearing houses that clear euro-denominated financial instruments above a certain threshold must be located in the euro area. However, as this is a monetary policy related rule, it seems unlikely that the EU's challenge will be upheld by the Court.

The third case refers to the 'bonus cap' in the Capital Requirements Directive (CRD), which is implementing the Basel III rules in European law. An amendment introduced by the European Parliament in the legislative process caps bonuses to one-times-salary (or two-times with shareholders' approval). The UK challenged this on grounds of the treaty base and procedure. The relevant provisions lack evidence and were not supported by the Commission's impact assessment, it is argued (p.88). However, the UK withdrew its challenge in November 2014 after it became apparent that it would not succeed in the European Court.

Assessment

The division of competences between the EU and the UK in financial services is considered in the Review to be "broadly appropriate" (p.5). But in deepening this assessment it is necessary to distinguish between matters of strategic reform and system development, versus matters of policy improvement.

At the strategic level, first of all, there is consensus on the need for the EU competence to ensure freedom of movement of payments and capital.

Secondly, as regards financial stability consensus also emerged that the pre-crisis system of fragmented national supervisory authorities was defective and had to be corrected with a new European system of financial supervision with several new EU agencies. It was also agreed, with strong UK backing, that there should be a single rulebook for regulatory standards. These reforms were rushed through in response to the emergency.

Thirdly, it became apparent that the supervisory system of the eurozone system itself needed further reinforcement, which has led to the banking union, in which the UK does not participate, but UK respondents to the Review show support for the eurozone itself.

Fourthly, complex issues regarding inter-relations between the EU financial market system and the banking union have emerged. Here, the UK has effectively negotiated a sophisticated system to control for non-discrimination in eurozone measures towards non-eurozone member states.

With respect to the details of EU financial sector regulation, respondents raise various criticisms about poor policy-making and inadequate impact assessments and consultations, which are concerns largely shared by other EU member states. The UK government has gone further in challenging the EU over three cases before the CJEU, but which most observers would not give (or have given) a good chance of success. The Review concludes that the UK should engage earlier and more effectively with the EU institutions, as well as with other member states.

The UK government itself still struggles to find a balanced approach to financial sector regulation, seven years after the start of the financial crisis. The UK's financial markets have continued to suffer from its light regulation approach, as illustrated recently (in November 2014, subsequent to publication of the Review) in the fines that had to be levied as a result of the huge foreign exchange rate-rigging practices.

Postscript. Since publication of the Review a new development is the capital markets union – an idea floated by the incoming President of the Commission, Jean-Claude Juncker. The possible content of this initiative will be of keen interest to the UK, and the incoming British Commissioner, Jonathan Hill, will be responsible for fleshing it out.

The evidence at a glance – financial services

Single market for financial services strategic for the City and the UK

EU regulatory approach radically reformed since 2008 crisis

More emphasis now on financial stability mechanisms, compared to past market-opening policies

Big challenge of reconciling single market with eurozone needs

UK secures non-participation in banking union and non-discrimination for non-euro member states

Continuing debate over policy details and Court cases

New capital market union idea to be explored, of interest to the UK

1.5 Free movement of people*

Britain's debate over the free movement of people within the EU has generated more heat than light. Nonetheless, it remains at the heart of why the UK attitude towards European integration has shifted from one of sceptical, but relatively benign neglect, to one of officially defensive hostility.[11] EU-watchers therefore eagerly awaited the government's Balance of Competences Review on this topic, to set out officially how free movement impacts Britain's national interests.[12] Publication of the Review was actually delayed for several months, divergent views were reported on its implicit conclusions, with Conservative ministers taking a more critical view of the status quo than their Liberal-Democrat colleagues.

A key reason why the free movement of people has become such a hot political issue for Britain is traced to its decision not to restrict access to its labour market in 2004, on the eve of the accession of the eight new member states. This meant that the spike in arrivals of nationals from these countries to the UK was much sharper than for many other member states that retained transitional restrictions. Between 2004 and 2012, the number of EU citizens resident in Britain more than doubled from 1.1 million to 2.3 million. Flows were significantly lower from Bulgaria and Romania, which received only staggered access to the UK labour market until January 2014. The more recent accession of Croatia has had no perceptible impact on immigration to the UK.

The report discusses the impact of free movement on Britain in terms of actual numbers, the impact on the welfare state, public order and the economy (broken down by sector, such as medicine, engineering and architecture). Helpfully, it includes a section on

---

* Section contributed by Hugo Brady.

[11] See, for example, David Cameron's intervention: "Free movement needs to be less free", *Financial Times*, 26 November 2013.

[12] The relevant EU legislation under review is the free movement Directive (2004); the Council Regulation on the free movement of workers (2011); a Directive on the enforcement of the free movement rights (adopted 2014); the EU's social security Regulation (2004) and the Directive on the mutual recognition of professional qualifications (latest amendments adopted in 2013).

how some 1.4-2.2 million Britons abroad make use of, and clearly benefit from free movement rights, such as British retirees in Spain and France, and how the EU's social security arrangements operate in this respect.[13] The analysis here focuses on the need for an even application of free- movement-related legislation across all member states. For example, the decades-long discrimination faced by non-native EU university lecturers in Italy is highlighted.

Broadly, the text supports the view that intra-EU migration is positive for the UK economy noting that, according to the UK's Office for National Statistics, some 60% of EU migrants coming to Britain to work already have job offers on arrival. The Russell Group – a UK research consortium that includes Britain's highest ranked universities – points out that non-UK EU nationals make up some 13.4% of researchers across its members (including Oxford, Cambridge, the LSE and Kings College London).

The City of London mounted a robust defence of intra-EU migration, noting that the average EU migrant pays around £23,000 per year in taxes while spending significantly on UK goods and services to the benefit of the wider economy, while being less likely to draw on public services such as the National Health Service. These facts are becoming more widely acknowledged in the UK with the result that the debate has moved on to focus more on the exportability of benefits, and questions of housing and school places. According to a study cited in the Review, some two-thirds of local councils in England expected to experience a shortage of school places by September 2016.

Public opinion in the UK has swung drastically against the free movement of people over the last decade, with a *YouGov* poll recording that nearly half the population was against the principle in 2013 from a position of two-thirds in favour in 2005. (UK unemployment remained low by historical standards, even during the 2008-2010 period of economic crisis, but more natives than migrants lost their jobs.) Many Britons feel that free movement is no longer fair; that it has become massively one-sided in terms of flows. EU/EEA immigration rose from 10% of UK net migration in

---

[13] The discrepancy between the estimated figures could be because many Britons spend part of their year abroad and part at home.

the 1970s to almost 40% by 2007. So-called 'benefit tourism' has become a totemic issue in the 'fairness' debate, since European migrants have the right to draw down universal benefits such as disability or children's allowance, if the children are not resident in the UK (see the postscript below).

The Review stresses the measures that the Cameron government has taken to restrict abuse of free movement within the bounds of the current legislation, noting also that other EU governments such as Germany have also taken action to combat 'poverty immigration' from elsewhere in the Union. The government has tightened up the immigration regulations that give effect to EU free movement rules in Britain. For example, since 1st April 2014, newly arrived EU migrants are no longer eligible for housing benefit in the UK. The UK has also made it harder for migrants who lose their 'right to reside' in Britain through long periods of economic inactivity to re-enter the country after a short interregnum. The 'right to reside' requirement was introduced to Britain's 'Habitual Residency Test' in 2004 as a means of managing an expected increase in EU migration. The criteria to qualify for the 'right to reside' are designed to ensure that only those migrants whose 'centre of interest' is the UK and who have some prospect of employment are eligible for benefits.

The residence test is currently the subject of an infraction proceeding against the UK taken by the Commission to the European Court of Justice. The Review notes hopefully that CJEU case law seems to support the arguments of Britain's lawyers that member states have the right to make access to benefits by EU nationals who are not economically active conditional upon them meeting the necessary requirements for obtaining a legal right of residence in the host member state (see below, the postscript).

Assessment

The report on free movement presents a far broader range of facts and analysis on this sensitive topic than is usually in evidence in Britain's debate on Europe. For the first time, for example, we read evidence from Britons exercising free movement rights abroad (there are 'expat' pensioners' associations with chapters in France and Spain). Moreover, various professional associations (such as the Architects Registration Board), regional governments and large firms are supporting the case for free movement.

On balance, the evidence points toward some changes to a free movement regime originally designed to operate between six broadly similar countries to better reflect a Union now far more diverse in incomes, social security arrangements, work expectations and migratory patterns.

But the Review's concluding passages lend conspicuous weight to the views of a single expert, who considers the UK's opening to Central and Eastern Europe in 2004 an historical error, arguing that free movement has dangerously unbalanced Britain's social contract. He argues that EU rules need to be re-cast to allow preference to be given to native workers in certain instances; that transitional arrangements for allowing new EU members access to Britain's labour market need to be based on more flexible criteria such as income disparity and economic convergence; and that governments should be free to impose caps on inward EU migration. This last 'cap' idea would clearly be unacceptable to the EU as a whole, and its retention in the conclusions of the Review is a reminder of the highly politicised context that surrounded the finalisation and delayed publication of this text.

Postscript. Subsequent to the publication of the Review there have been two significant developments. First, the CJEU made a ruling in the Dano case (C-333/13) in November 2014 that supported national competences in deciding upon residence requirements and their significance in determining eligibility for certain social benefits. While the case in point was in Germany, the ruling is supporting rather than undermining national competences in this field, and the British Prime Minister noted that it was "simple common sense".

Second, on 28th November the Prime Minister set out in detail what he hopes to negotiate with the EU in order to control immigration from the EU more strictly, without breaking the principle of free movement of people. These proposals include:

- denial of tax credits, and housing benefits for EU citizens before four years of residence;
- removal of job seekers if they find no job within six months;
- stronger measures to deport criminals;
- no payment of child benefits for children resident abroad;
- longer waiting period for free movement for citizens of future acceding states.

The detailed legal analysis of these proposals are a mixed bag of measures, where in some cases the UK is entitled to take freely as a matter on national competence, of others that would be more difficult in that they require legislation by the EU decided by qualified majority, and some that would seem to be virtually impossible in requiring treaty change to be decided unanimously by all member states and ratified by all national parliaments.[14]

This is the only instance so far where the Prime Minster has set out an operational agenda for negotiation or re-negotiation with the EU, hinting that some solutions might be either through EU-wide legislation, or new special provisions for the UK. It is significant that these are the Prime Minister's proposals, not those of the coalition government with the Liberal Democrats, signalling only partial support from them. As a consequence, the proposals would only be formally addressed to the EU after the 2015 general election, and only then if there were an outright Conservative Party government. Reactions from Brussels indicate a willingness to examine these requests, but it would seem that negotiations can await the next British government.

The evidence at a glance – free movement of people

Competence for free movement fundamental in EU as a whole

Sharply contested views in UK between interest groups and political parties

2008 enlargement caused immigration spike in UK, heavily impacting public opinion

UK residents in EU states equal number of other EU residents in UK

CJEU case helpful in clarifying national competences for residence and thence access to certain social benefits

Cameron announces operational reform or re-negotiation proposals, some within existing national competences, others requiring EU agreement of varying difficulty

---

[14] For a detailed review see Steve Peers, "EU Law Analysis" (http://eulawanalysis.blogspot.co.uk/2014/11/the-nine-labours-of-cameron-analysis-of.html), 28 November 2014.

1.6 Competition and consumer policies

This Review covers both competition policy for which the Treaty provides the EU with 'exclusive competence' for "establishing the competition rules necessary for the functioning of the internal market" (Article 3, TFEU), and consumer policy for which the Treaty provides for "shared competence" (Article 4, TFEU).

The competition policy divides between anti-trust provisions (Articles 101-106, TFEU) and state aid rules (Articles 107-109, TFEU). The competition rules prohibit anti-competitive agreements between undertakings and the abusive conduct of dominant undertakings.

The state aid rules prohibit such aids in general, but with exemptions allowed for several categories of case: aid to small and medium-sized enterprises (SMEs); social aid to disabled people; regional aid; environmental aid; and research and innovation spending. These provisions originated in the Treaty of Rome and have not been materially changed since then. However, they have been further elaborated through numerous case decisions by the CJEU, and a merger control competence was introduced in 1989.

For state aid, respondents gave evidence that there was broad agreement in principle on the current balance of competence (p.42). The Commission proposed a reform package in 2012, which resulted in Council regulations in 2013 that enlarged the exemptions categories and adopted procedures to handle complaints faster and more predictably. The Commission has also revised its 'Guidelines' to enable it to concentrate on cases that have the biggest impact of the internal market. There has been debate whether the minimum size (actually €200,000) of aid should be raised before EU controls. The UK coalition government and the Commission have agreed that this would not be really helpful, and that extending exemption categories might be a better approach.

For competition policy the Review explains the relationship between the EU's competences and national competition policies, and the UK's Competition Act of 2008 is a case in point. Member states retain considerable autonomy in their enforcement of competition rules, and notably over cases that have no impact on inter-state trade, for which the EU has no competence. However, the UK's Competition Act was deliberately modelled on EU law in order to ease the burden for businesses so that they would not have to respect two different regimes. The investigative and sanction powers of the UK authorities are similar to those of the Commission.

Since 2004 the enforcement of EU anti-trust provisions has been reformed to allow greater decentralisation of enforcement to national competition authorities. There is considerable flexibility in the extent to which individual member states may take up these possibilities, reflecting the varying strengths of national administrations. Stakeholders and respondents were clearly supporting the EU's competence in this area as corresponding to the national interest, in making markets more effective and dynamic and ensuring a level playing field. The de-centralisation of enforcement was seen to be "an exemplar of subsidiarity working well in practice" (p. 39).

The level of fines on companies infringing competition rules can be very high; up to 10% of worldwide turnover, with both *Intel* and *Microsoft* having been fined over €1 billion for abuse of dominance.

The competence for merger control is shared clearly between the EU and member states, with the EU only to act where the mergers have an 'EU dimension'.

Competition policy has an important international perspective, with the EU model having proved a significant factor in the expansion to 128 countries of competition policy regimes. In this regard the Review notes that "the EU system has proved to be a more popular transplant than the US one, the only feasible alternative, and many overseas competition regimes are modelled on EU provisions" (p.64).

For consumer policy its legal foundations came much later with the Single European Act in 1987 and the Maastricht Treaty in 1993. In this case of 'shared competence' between the EU and member states there is much scope for debate about how the principles of subsidiarity and proportionality should be applied. There has been a lively debate about whether EU consumer rules should specify minimum or maximum standards. Minimum standards allow for more flexibility in setting higher national standards where desired, and many UK stakeholders supported this view. The case for maximum standards is based on the need to avoid fragmenting the internal market. As a result of negotiations on this issue in response to the Commission Green Paper of 2007, the outcome was that most provisions should be harmonised at the maximum level, but with important exemptions to be allowed for certain categories of goods and services.

A case in 2013 in which the Commission proposed to regulate the packaging of olive oil on the tables of restaurants illustrates the state of the debate over subsidiarity in the consumer policy domain. The Commission had been lobbied by producers into proposing that olive oil had to be displayed in the original producer's packaging to prevent consumers being afflicted by substandard olive oil. There was instant public outcry that this regulation was not really needed, and the proposal was rapidly withdrawn. This conforms to the doctrine advanced by the Commission nowadays that the EU should do fewer small things, and concentrate on big issues.

Assessment

The Review reports strong consensus on the need for centralised competences at the EU level for both anti-trust polices and the control of state aid. In the case of the UK there is good coherence between its national policies and those of the EU, with UK policies being modelled on those of the EU.

Consumer policy is also an essential feature of an effective single market, and in ensuring that it works well for consumers and society as a whole.

In all three cases – anti-trust, state aids and consumer policies – there has been lively debate about how to optimise the subsidiarity principle. In each case there is evidence of policy refinement or reform that includes elements of enhanced decentralisation, while in all cases there is a reasoned limitation to how far this should go.

An interesting international aspect is that the EU model of competition policy is the one most emulated by other countries developing their own policies.

> **The evidence at a glance – competition and consumer policies**
>
> *Stakeholders strongly support EU competition policy competence over cases affecting inter-state trade*
>
> *2004 reforms provide for greater decentralisation of enforcement,*
>
> *'Exemplar' of subsidiarity working well in practice*
>
> *2013 reforms of 'Guidelines' on state aid to focus on big cases*
>
> *For consumer policy balance of opinion favourable, with nuances*
>
> *Much copying internationally of the EU model as 'best practice'*

1.7 Foreign trade and investment

Trade policy is a core exclusive competence of the EU. There are nonetheless a number of second-order issues that concern the extent of this competence for both trade and investment. The report goes into these second-order issues in detail. It also reviews the hypothetical alternatives, if the UK wished to secede from the EU's trade policy, which would necessarily mean secession from the EU, since wholesale repatriation of this competence is inconceivable.

While the original competence of the EU (or earlier, the EEC) essentially concerned trade in goods, the importance of trade in services and trade-related aspects of intellectual property rights has been growing to the point that much case law of the European Court of Justice has enlarged the EU's competence in these fields. This led to a tidying up of these particular competence questions in the Treaty of Lisbon, which also opened up investment protection as a field with some new exclusive competence for the EU.

For services, the Treaty of Lisbon clarifies the EU's exclusive competence to negotiate agreements over trade in services as defined in the General Agreement on Trade in Services (GATS) texts of the WTO. Similarly, for intellectual property rights the EU is now competent for negotiations in the field covered by the Trade-Related Aspects of Intellectual Property Rights (TRIPS) texts of the WTO. While the extent of these competences had earlier been the subject of much uncertainty alongside many ad hoc rulings of the Court of Justice, the extension and clarification of EU competences did not meet with particular objections from stakeholders contributing evidence to the review.

The field of investment protection has so far been occupied by bilateral investment protection treaties ('BITs'), of which the member states have in force no fewer than 1,200 examples, and the UK on its own has 96. The case for an EU competence here is for simplification, clarity and a level playing field. However, the precise extent of the EU's new post-Lisbon competence in this field is still to be clarified in two respects, namely whether it concerns only foreign direct investment or all investment, and whether it concerns only investment liberalisation agreements or also protection of actual investments. The Review considers that resolution of these issues will require rulings by the European Court of Justice.

A related question is whether future EU agreements in this field will be 'exclusive' or 'mixed' agreements, with member states retaining greater say in the legislative process in the latter case. There remain ambiguities over the extent of the EU's competence to negotiate on behalf of member states in areas that remain national competences. Since the EU-Japan FTA mandate of 2012 the Council has started using a 'double-decision' mechanism whereby the Council authorises the Commission, in two separate acts, to negotiate issues of its exclusive competences on the one hand, and on the other its competences 'shared' with member states. The report remarks that the Commission does not support this mechanism, but goes along with it.

The Review shows that stakeholders felt that trade and investment promotion, as opposed to trade policy, should remain a national competence, although the EU could provide a useful supporting role in this regard. This position would be considered uncontroversial in the EU as a whole, and there are no proposals for legal competence transfer in this field.

The alternatives. The Review discusses six hypothetical alternatives for how trade policy could be handled from outside the EU (which are crucial to the question of secession, to which we return in the final chapter).

i) *Going it alone.* The UK would have a 'third country relationship' with the EU, as any WTO member state that does not make a preferential agreement with it. Customs duties would be re-introduced between the UK and the EU, thus diminishing trade flows. The UK would be free to negotiate free trade agreements (FTAs) with other countries, but whether it would be able to negotiate better deals than the EU is open to doubt, since its bargaining clout would be so much smaller.

ii) *The UK to make an FTA with the EU for trade in goods.* This would require that complex 'rules of origin' be introduced, to prove that UK exports to the EU would have been sufficiently 'made in the UK'. Compliance costs, including a lot of 'red tape', would amount to a significant non-tariff barrier.

iii) *The UK makes a more comprehensive FTA with the EU.* There would be additional provisions for services and investment, like the EU-Korea agreement. This would still require the 'rules of origin' red tape, without guaranteeing full access to the single market.

iv) *The UK joins the EU customs union from the outside, like Turkey.* In this case the UK would still be bound by the EU's external trade policy, without having fully guaranteed access to the single market.

v) *The UK joins the European Economic Area (EEA), like Norway.* The EU would have the freedom to make its own trade policy with third countries, and would retain full guaranteed access to the single market. However, it would lose 'sovereignty' by having no say in the ongoing development of single market policies.

vi) *The UK makes a more flexible agreement with the EU, like Switzerland.* This consists of a bundle of agreements that would almost amount to being in the EEA. This was the ad hoc patching up of the system after Switzerland voted in a referendum against joining the EEA. The Swiss model is criticised within the EU for its cherry-picking, complex nature; it is thus unlikely that the EU would be willing to replicate it for the UK.

Assessment

The large majority of stakeholders responding to the call for evidence expressed the view that the existing competences of the EU in the field of trade and investment were "broadly appropriate", or that they saw "no advantages in altering the current balance of competences in this area", although there were a few dissenting opinions. The Review traced the evolution of the EU's competences, including the provisions of the Lisbon Treaty that clarified, updated and somewhat extended these competences, such as in the services area. These developments were not contested, however.

There remain concerns of a more detailed character. These involve the fine-tuning of the competences of the EU alongside those of the member states, notably in the area of 'shared' competences. In addition, there are calls for greater transparency and more comprehensive impact assessments to be made by the Commission in relation to ongoing negotiations for new free trade agreements. The present author concurs with that, having in mind the new model of Deep and Comprehensive Free Trade Agreements (DCFTAs) with countries of the European neighbourhood, where huge blocks of EU legislation have been included for compliance by the partner states, with no evident assessment of where the costs of compliance might be unreasonably high.

Since any basic repatriation of this competence to member states is out of the question, the alternatives have to involve the hypothesis of secession by the UK. The report does therefore thoroughly review the landscape of alternatives, but on inspection they all reveal serious disadvantages or risks attached to them. Finally, the Review considers that the EU, with the UK outside it, would be more protectionist, and more willing to use trade defence instruments, including against the UK.

"The evidence received for stakeholders generally suggests that the balance of competences in this area allows the UK to achieve results that are in the national interest" (p.6).

The evidence at a glance - foreign trade and investment

Core exclusive competence of EU in trade policy not contested

No advantages in changing current balance of competence

No good options for trade policy regimes in the event of secession

2. Sectoral policies

2.1 Transport*

Transport is a competence shared between the EU and its member states, which means that both may adopt legally binding acts in this policy area but the latter only insofar as the former has not exercised its competences or has explicitly ceased to do so. Seen through this prism, the Department for Transport, which drew up this particular Review, rightly uses a broad definition of EU competence in the transport context, namely that it is about everything deriving from EU law that affects what happens to transport in the UK. As such, this Review links in with issues that are covered in others, for example those on the standardisation of goods, customs security procedures, environmental standards, employment issues, etc.

In the transport field the Council acts by qualified majority voting, meaning that the UK, like any other single member state, does not have the power of veto. The evidence collected suggests that, generally speaking, this is not problematic. British domestic transport policy and experience is seen as one of the models for EU proposals on transport market reforms and liberalisation: "[t]he UK has been a leading advocate for the development of the single market in transport across all modes, and in the 1980s and 1990s led efforts to break down national barriers within the EU to the provision of transport services across borders and within other countries, to the benefit of UK businesses and consumers" (p.13).

While respondents perceive the balance of competence to heavily favour the EU in legislation, they are generally happy with the current legislative framework and do not advocate adjustment of that balance. It was acknowledged that EU-level legislation can achieve (and has achieved) much more than UK legislation can do on its own.

EU transport policies concern all modes: road, rail, air, water, maritime, ports. The Review draws attention to some striking achievements, notably in the civil aviation sector. The

---

* Section contributed by Steven Blockmans.

UK's largest low-cost carrier declared: "EasyJet is a product of the EU's deregulation of the European aviation market. Without deregulation we would not exist" (p.24). A graph shows how the average fare paid by UK-resident passengers on intra-EU flights had fallen by half over the last 15 years, whereas trans-Atlantic fares had barely fallen (p.25).

The British opt-out from the Schengen area is identified as posing a challenge: "The prospect of new rail services from points of departure across the EU has created a significant challenge for both UK and Schengen border control authorities in identifying border control solutions for rail which support the rapid transit of high speed intercity services" (p.19).

While the balance of competences in transport is generally strongly supported, so too are the principles of subsidiarity and proportionality. There is broad support for the leading role of the EU in international agreements as it provides consistency, standardisation and a level playing field for markets in all 28 EU member states and relevant third countries, which in turn provides greater legal certainty. The EU is perceived as being able to amplify the voices of the component member states (e.g. in international organisations) and extract greater commitments to liberalisation of global markets and fair competition from third countries like China or the US.

The UK government was, however, keen to reiterate its stance that any EU statement in international organisations on issues where competence is shared between the EU and the member states must make clear that it is delivered on behalf of the member states and the EU. To avoid 'representation creep', the UK also takes a more restrictive view than the Commission of the extent to which EU Delegations may deliver EU statements in line with Article 17 TEU (see below, on Foreign Policy).

There is also frustration among stakeholders about EU initiatives to legislate in areas where regulation at the global level would be preferable to creating regional systems that lead to losses of global competitiveness for European industries (e.g. maritime port services and the Emissions Trading System in aviation); but also awareness that global agreements may be unachievable.

When it comes to non-intra-European issues and greater scope for national handling of purely domestic issues, some stakeholders (e.g. in the tourism sector) urge the EU to legislate with a lighter touch, or not at all. The greater body of evidence from across all transport modes shows frustration where the creation of a single market has been held back by ineffective implementation. EU mechanisms used to implement change were often felt to create additional costs and regulatory burdens, or lack enforcement by the European Commission across the 28 member states.

While British industry recognises the value of common assessment procedures, operating standards and technical product standards in helping to reduce red tape and costs in manufacturing, in spurring innovation, facilitating interoperability and increasing the potential for exports through opening markets in other member states, and that these benefits would not exist across the EU without EU action, there was also concern at the perceived use of common standards in other fields, such as safety, environment or social policy, to claw back market freedoms and allow the potential imposition of national barriers, possibly in a protectionist way. Many of the responses to the call for evidence were centred on social standards in road transport.

As concerns the issue of better regulation, a general message from stakeholders is that the European Commission should recognise the maturity of the EU as an organisation, focusing less on making proposals for new legislation and concentrating more on enforcement of existing legislation. The Review also states that nearly all stakeholders feel that before making proposals for legislation, the Commission should undertake more openly evidenced impact assessments that set out clearly the potential costs and benefits.

Assessment. The UK has generally been a leading advocate for the development of a single market in transport services, which is at the core of the EU's common transport policy. This Review suggests that the current balance of EU competences in the field of transport is broadly right. Evidence from experts shows that there is broad support for the EU common transport policy to continue yielding those benefits for Britain. There is no consensus that individual areas of EU transport law should fall outside the competence of the EU in the future. However, there is a general view among stakeholders that the way to achieve further liberalisation is, in many cases, through more effective implementation and enforcement of existing legislation rather than through continually seeking new legislation. There is evidence of frustration with some of the social, safety and environmental rules, especially where these impinge on purely domestic transport without any international dimension. The concerns expressed about new regulatory burdens and costs mean that there is still much work to be done to find the right level of legislative prescription that achieves the stated aims without imposing disproportionate costs or prohibiting innovation.

The evidence at a glance – transport

UK driver of single market in transport, influential policy model

Striking deregulation results, e.g. UK passenger air fares in EU cut by half

EU competence broadly right, strongly supported by stakeholders

EU policy in transport judged 'mature'

Need for enforcement of present laws, more than for new ones

2.2 Energy*

The UK is both the third largest producer and consumer of energy in the European Union. However, while final energy consumption is picking up as a consequence of economic recovery, domestic production of crude oil, natural gas and hard coal continues to decrease rapidly.[15] Since three-quarters of the UK's energy mix are still based on fossil fuels, import dependency is rising quickly. In fact, while the UK has mostly been a net exporter of energy since 1980, it became a net importer again in 2004 and by 2012 imported some 42% of its energy needs. In addition, the heavy dependence on fossil fuels causes the UK to remain the second largest emitter

---

* Section contributed by Arno Behrens.

[15] For example, UK natural gas production decreased from 98 million tonnes of oil equivalent (Mtoe) in 2000 to 35 Mtoe in 2012. Similarly, UK crude oil and natural gas liquids (NGL) production decreased from 128 Mtoe in 2000 to 46 Mtoe in 2012.

of greenhouse gases in the EU, with emissions again on the rise since 2011. Finally, the UK – like other EU member states – has been facing increasing oil and electricity prices, in particular since 2003, despite full liberalisation of electricity and gas markets in the late 1990s. Concerns about energy prices and competition, security of energy supplies and climate change have thus increased the attention given to energy policy in the UK over the past decade, *inter alia* leading to the establishment of its own government department in October 2008.

Most of these concerns, however, are not UK specific but have been shared by the majority of other EU member states. From this point of view it is not surprising that the UK was a major driver of EU energy policy, in particular with the 2005 Hampton Court informal European summit being considered as a major new impetus for a more common approach to energy at the EU level. In fact, it was this summit that led to the European Commission Green Paper on "A European strategy for sustainable, competitive and secure energy" in 2006, which in turn laid the foundations for the EU's energy and climate change package and the related 2020 targets agreed upon in 2007 – the centrepiece of EU energy and climate policy to this day.

While the UK has particular interests as a major producer of energy sources (some of which are well guarded in the Lisbon Treaty, see below), it also benefits from a more European approach towards the European energy market. This is particularly the case regarding further integration of the internal market, which has always been at the heart of the UK approach towards EU energy policy. The energy review is very clear in this respect, highlighting the creation of a level playing field for competition within the single market as a key benefit for the UK, together with the facilitation of cross-border trading, enhancing interconnectivity and improving security of supply as a result of physical market integration.

Although the internal energy market was to be 'completed' by 2014, slow or partial implementation of the 'third energy package' by some member states means that many barriers to competition are likely to remain for a while. This is rightly criticised in the energy review, which calls for more effective monitoring by the Commission and appropriate action (infringement procedures) where member states fail to implement existing legislation. The report also mentions that the UK experienced disadvantages from over-implementation ('gold plating') of EU internal energy market legislation in some areas, and indeed, the UK currently faces no infringement procedures, either under the second or the third energy package.

However, the report does not mention the fact that the UK itself has more recently deviated from its market-oriented approach by adopting the Energy Act in 2013, which includes *inter alia* provisions for so-called Contracts for Difference (CfDs) as well as for capacity markets. Such provisions will most likely not only increase electricity prices in the future, but – worse than that – will increasingly lead to the replacement of market rules with national regulations as the basis for investment decisions. Although in October 2014 the European Commission found that price support in the form of CfD for the new Hinkley Point nuclear power station did not contradict EU state aid rules, such measures are designed as national policy instruments, thus further undermining the internal energy market and efforts to deliver cost-effective solutions through competition.

The Review also reflects the strong interest of UK stakeholders in the security of energy supplies. In this respect, the main emphasis of the report is on infrastructure and the exploitation of domestic energy sources. Regarding infrastructure, an EU-wide approach was found to be particularly effective regarding common rules for trans-boundary interconnection projects and EU funding through the Connecting Europe Facility, from which the UK will also be able to benefit. The first list of 'Projects of Common Interest' includes several UK clustered electricity interconnection projects, a smart grid project and gas projects involving Northern Ireland.

Enthusiasm for a pan-European approach to energy infrastructure was counterbalanced by scepticism towards EU action regarding the exploitation of oil and gas reserves in the North Sea and the refining of fossil fuels. Article 194 (TFEU) of the Lisbon Treaty clearly protects a member state's right "to determine the conditions for exploiting its energy resources, its choice between different energy sources and the general structure of its energy supply". Fears of upstream stakeholders are therefore more oriented towards EU safety legislation and changes to the technical Network Codes. Similarly, the UK energy sector seems to see no need for additional EU legislation on shale gas exploitation, although environmental groups noted that existing national and EU legislation was not sufficient to mitigate potential environmental impacts.

As a result of this dichotomy, the Review reflects a contradiction between those who criticise the fact that security of supply issues had not been given sufficient weight at EU level and those who believe national solutions are more appropriate to secure supplies. Declining domestic reserves and increasing import dependence may shift future preferences further towards strengthening the EU component in security of supply policies.

Since environment and climate change have already been dealt with in the context of a separate review (see the next section), the one for energy focuses mainly on renewable energy sources, energy efficiency, and carbon capture and storage. Not surprisingly, the renewables sector and environmental groups argue that EU targets and policies had helped the UK to advance further on renewable energy and energy efficiency than it would otherwise have done in the absence of such actions.

But the Review also correctly identifies the need for more policy coherence between multiple EU targets (i.e. climate, renewables and energy efficiency). In this respect, the report reflects the debate about whether technology-specific targets are a cost-effective means to achieve emissions reductions. In particular, the focus on renewables is said to distort the market by undermining the carbon price signal and reducing incentives to invest in carbon capture and storage technologies (and other low carbon energy sources), which have large potential in the UK.

Assessment

Overall, the energy review provides a balanced overview of the successes and failures of EU energy policy, as well as its advantages and disadvantages for the UK. Looking at the key challenges that lie ahead in the energy field from the viewpoint of UK stakeholders (see below), the Review concludes that more EU energy policy could benefit the UK in addressing these challenges.

Cases made for the UK to repatriate energy policy issues from the competences of the EU are scarce.

Three prime challenges are identified. The first concerns the impact of growing global energy demand and geopolitical developments in the security of EU and UK energy supplies. As UK import dependency rises, the UK will increasingly benefit from more interconnections, EU funding for infrastructure development and increasing solidarity between member states, as laid down in the TFEU. The interdependence of member states calls for more collective action, in particular regarding network development and opening up markets, but also regarding a more coherent external action. Fears over EU intervention in national energy mixes are unfounded as the EU has no competence over such matters, leaving it up to the UK to exploit indigenous energy sources such as shale gas, nuclear or (clean) coal.

The second challenge relates to the internal market as the means to secure a key objective of EU energy policy from the British standpoint, namely to assure a level playing field for competition, notably in a context in which there is actually an increasing disparity of energy prices between individual member states, with consequences for UK competitiveness. Concerns voiced in the report about the slow and partial implementation of internal market legislation in some member states are thus in stark contrast to the UK government's recent initiatives to introduce more national measures, including Contracts for Difference (CfDs) and capacity mechanisms, which will lead to further fragmentation of the internal market. This is counterintuitive to the review's findings that a well-functioning internal energy market should place downward pressure on gas and electricity prices. More EU rather than less, i.e. fully functioning liberalised EU-wide electricity and gas markets, is what UK stakeholders seem to prefer. The UK should thus be leading this development in its own interest. This can best be done proactively from within the EU. A hypothetical EU secession, on the other hand, would leave the UK without the possibility to influence internal market legislation, even if it still had to implement it should it remain part of the single market.

Postscript. Subsequent to publication of the energy review, negotiations over the EU's '2030 framework' were finally concluded in October 2014. The UK government initially supported a single greenhouse gas emissions reduction target in the context of the EU negotiations over its 2030 framework for climate and energy policies, which in turn is an essential input into the global climate change negotiations currently underway. While the UK advocated the adoption of a unilateral EU-wide greenhouse gas emissions reduction target of 40% for 2030, it was opposed to specifying particular ways in which this target must be achieved. In order to preserve flexibility and allow member states to choose the best and most cost-effective way to meet their emissions reduction commitments, the UK government did not initially support either a renewable energy target to be included in the 2030 framework, or a binding energy efficiency target.

The final agreement reached in October 2014 was different, but still seems to be a good compromise for the UK. It includes a binding 40% greenhouse gas emissions reduction target (to be translated into binding targets at member state level for the non-ETS sectors), but downgraded the 27% renewables target to an obligation only binding on the EU level. What this means precisely is still unclear, but there will certainly not be binding commitments for member states to reach national targets. The 27% energy efficiency target also remains indicative and thus neither binding on the EU nor on the member state level. This compromise is favourable to the UK position. In particular, it steers a path between those member states that advocated a less ambitious climate target on the one hand, and those that favoured higher and binding obligations on renewables and energy efficiency on the other. While the UK could surely pursue an ambitious national climate policy – also outside of the EU – more cost-effective solutions can be found through concerted action (e.g. through the EU's Emissions Trading System, pioneered by the UK as a pilot national scheme from 2002). The UK actually received much of what it wanted in the 2030 framework agreement reached in October 2014.

The evidence at a glance – energy

Competence justified by common concerns for security of supplies and single market

UK a main driver for EU policy, especially now that own oil and gas production declines

UK drive for fully liberalised and integrated internal market for efficiency and security

Some UK policies are less liberal, but accepted under EU state aid policy

New 2030 EU framework reforms agreed to boost renewables, but with details left to member states, as the UK wanted

---

2.3 Environment and climate change[*]

The review of the development of environmental and climate change legislation gives a clear grounding to consider the objectives and balance of legislation developed so far, and the options for its further development.

The major turning point for facilitating EU environmental legislation came with the 1987 Single European Act, which introduced qualified majority (QMV) voting into the legislative process, including for environmental legislation. During that period, the UK was under considerable pressure from other member states on environmental issues. It was no coincidence that Prime Minister Margaret Thatcher's promotion of the long-term issue of climate change emerged at a time when the pressures in favour of QMV voting were building up in the Council.

The climate change issue has distinctive characteristics, including complicated interactions, in particular with energy policy and its shared legal competences in the EU. So the balance of competences for climate change is best addressed separately, even if the legal basis used for much of the EU legislation in this area has been environmental.

Environment. The Review correctly identifies that EU environmental legislation started with the purpose of protecting

---

[*] Section contributed by Michael Wriglesworth.

the proper functioning of the single market. The fundamental issue is over how to achieve environmental objectives, while ensuring a level playing field for competition within the single market. Whereas the single market objective is clearly a UK priority, the competitive consequences of uneven application of environmental (and social) legislation within the single market are not well understood by the general public or by some in industry. Germany, also a strong supporter of the single market, has often taken the lead in enacting and promoting strong environmental (and social) legislation, while not wanting to be placed at a competitive disadvantage as a result.

The Review reflects the strong interest in environmental protection in the UK, even if there is less agreement on how this is best achieved, locally, or through EU and international cooperation. In the consultation some respondents considered that lack of trans-boundary impact is a sufficient reason for the EU to abstain from individual actions. Other respondents advocated reliance on the principles of subsidiarity and/or proportionality. However, there was no case made for the UK to repatriate *environment* from the competences of the EU as a general proposition. There was strong recognition of the benefits of setting high environmental standards at EU level, and of extending such approaches more widely, at UN level and in trade agreements, often using the powerful principle of the 'technical equivalence' of standards.

A contentious issue concerns the protection of natural habitats, and related assessments of environmental impact. At the heart of the former are different views about the value of protecting the natural environment. In the past there has been some contention between the Commission and the UK about the implementation of the Environmental Impact Assessment (EIA) Directive, relating to a series of projects, including motorways and a major oil pipeline project in Scotland. The tension here is that the UK has led in promoting the EIA approach, but fallen foul of implementing the EU directive incorporating these principles.

This is a familiar UK problem, when a UK-supported approach becomes burdensome in its implementation at the EU level. There is a balance of judgements here between welcoming implementation of UK-initiated principles, and recognising that implementation at the EU level will inevitably become rather more bureaucratic than a UK national approach.

The Review picks out important tensions between the interests of larger exporting companies in the setting of standards within the single market, and SMEs' concerns that increased legislation can lead to administrative burdens they can ill afford. Linked to this are the twin concerns that implementation of EU legislation is both over-elaborate ('gold-plated') in the case of the UK, and less stringently implemented in some other member states. These issues have parallels in other areas, such as in social, health and safety legislation. The Review correctly identifies that a balance needs to be struck between these tensions, and that this balance might be improved.

The UK originally led in developing the 'environmental quality' approach to setting standards, based on the view that the environmental impact of emissions is key in making cost-effective choices to achieve high environmental standards, such as in air and water quality. The Review sets out the important development and implementation in the EU of the 'precautionary principle', and the approach grounded in the EU treaty that the polluter must pay. As part of the precautionary principle the Review sets out another important contribution that the UK has helped to make in developing environmental and health legislation; namely assessing and managing risk once hazards have been identified.

This is helpful for resolving tensions over some of the most contentious environmental legislation, namely the REACH Regulation to control hazardous chemicals, where intrinsic hazard is approached by a process of risk assessment and risk management. The UK initiated the EU process that led to agreement of the REACH, but this is often used as an example of EU legislation that is burdensome for companies, especially SMEs. However, REACH does not seem to be an example of the UK over-elaborating, or 'gold-plating', legislation in implementation. REACH is actually an example of legislative simplification, replacing a number of directives and regulations with a single system to control dangerous chemicals. Registration is centralised in a single system through the EU Chemical Agency, to allow free movement of chemicals within the single market. There is a case now being considered, however, for the implementation of

REACH to be further simplified, especially to make its registration and reporting obligations less burdensome for SMEs.

A major concern about the REACH approach for international chemical companies has been that once implemented in Europe, an equivalent approach to REACH should be adopted in the US, and this has in fact started to happen.

Overall, the Review makes the case for the EU to further apply the principles of proportionality and subsidiarity to environmental policy and legislation, which the Netherlands is also supporting, rather than identifying scope to repatriate to the UK legal competences in this environmental area.

Climate change. The major characteristic of the climate change issue is the need for international agreement and cooperation, even though this is proving difficult to achieve. The key issues - mitigation of greenhouse gas emissions, transfer of technology, and adaptation to expected impacts of climate change - all need agreed global responses, both to be effective, and to ensure that less developed countries are also able to contribute to global effort.

The Review recognises that the need to agree actions and cooperation in implementation calls for shared competences, both at global UNFCCC level, and particularly in the EU. Specifically, the EU acts as a team in UNFCCC negotiations, first agreeing its own positions by EU consensus, before moving on to the more challenging UN level.

The EU, and within it the UK, have a long record of leadership roles on these issues, and the UK has been the more effective by being an active member of the EU team within the UNFCCC. This is recognised in the Review, and expressed as UK influence being amplified by the EU. The concern of a minority of respondents that the UK's voice might not be adequately reflected in EU decisions is not borne out by the record of the EU's role in the UNFCCC, nor in EU legislation that has been agreed. Partly, this derives from the initiative of former Prime Minister Thatcher to put the UK in a leading role, both in UNFCCC and in the EU, including nomination of the then head of the UK Meteorological Service as the first chair of the Intergovernmental Panel on Climate Change (IPCC), as part of the UN process.

A fundamental aspect of climate change policy is how closely it interacts with energy policy, for which there is also shared competence between member states and the EU. In particular, the crucial choice of fuel mix, and so carbon emission, is specifically reserved for member states. Germany and the UK have led in ensuring that EU team effort on climate change will not compromise these national energy priorities. These two member states started with rather different views on the suitability of emissions trading as the central instrument of EU policy in implementing climate change obligations, but they were able to resolve their differences.

The EU's Emission Trading System (ETS) is the lynchpin of concerted action on climate change, giving the European Commission important standing in relation to member state strategies. To prepare an ETS allocation plan, a member state must prepare a mitigation strategy for all of its emissions, and these strategies need to add up to the EU's overall commitment. Industry lobbying resulted in over-allocation of emission allowances, which, compounded by the recession, has slashed the price of CO_2 allowances. This does not negate, however, the strategic importance of putting a price on carbon, which principle the UK asserted, at the UN and EU levels.

A fundamental point for the UK in climate change policy is that for its major interests to be protected, it is vital to remain engaged as a full member state. A current example is the UK's concern (shared by other member states) not to have renewable energy targets imposed as part of a 2030 climate change and energy package. A UK half-engaged, say by remaining within the EU single market, but not as a full member state, might find itself having to meet EU requirements without being able to represent its major concerns in the course of the EU's legislative process.

Assessment

The Review has shown that the UK has been both a major driver and a beneficiary of EU environmental policy, and a leader on climate change policy, both within the EU and at UN level. The consequences of a hypothetical UK secession from the EU would compromise the UK's ability to lead and steer effectively, whilst leaving it vulnerable to being required to contribute to EU internal and international commitments as a condition of continued membership of the single market, but without having a say in what is agreed.

Many in the UK welcome the drive to improve EU environmental standards. This has been in many fields, including coastal bathing and drinking water, urban air quality associated with single market standards for vehicles and fuels, waste disposal and ground water protection. Improved environmental quality in these fields is on the record, as it is for dangerous substances and installations ('Seveso' Directives), and for chemicals.

There is an issue over the detail and reach of EU environmental legislation, but here the UK can surely join with its EU partners in seeking regulatory simplification, whilst maintaining high standards. Then there will be the further opportunity to join with its EU partners in taking these high environmental standards to the global market place.

Postscript. As reported in the previous section, subsequent to publication of the Review, there were important developments in October 2014 with agreement on the EU's '2030 framework' for both energy and climate change policies.

The evidence at a glance – environment and climate change

The UK is a leader of climate change policy in EU and through the EU at UN level

The UK is both a major driver and beneficiary of EU environmental policy

Need for subsidiarity and proportionality in environmental regulations

Case for simplifying some regulations (e.g. REACH for chemicals) for SMEs

2.4 Agriculture*

Agriculture is a field in which the EU has extensive competences. The Common Agricultural Policy (CAP) combines a greater degree of regulatory harmonisation, common financing and economic integration than any other area of EU activity. Moreover, it is a policy that British governments have always considered to be disadvantageous to UK interests. Since agriculture is less important to the British economy than in other member states, and British farms are generally larger in size, the UK receives relatively little benefit from CAP rules designed to support market prices and farmers' incomes. For British commentators agricultural policy is often perceived as the most negative aspect of EU membership, both from a general economic point of view (transfer of resources to inefficient producers) and financially (for many years agriculture took the largest share of the EU budget, and for the period 2014-2020 it still takes 36%). In fact, the high level of EU expenditure on agriculture, combined with Britain's limited receipts, was and continues to be the main justification for the UK's demand for a budgetary 'rebate'.

Against this background, it is not surprising that the Review contains strong criticism of the EU's agricultural policy. The majority of respondents argued that "the CAP remains misdirected, cumbersome, costly and bureaucratic", or that "the CAP's objectives remain unclear and the criteria for allocation of funding are irrational and disconnected from what the policy should be aiming to achieve" (p.5).

Nevertheless, there is "a recognition that the CAP) has changed significantly, particularly over the past 30 years. The most damaging and trade-distorting elements have been removed and the UK has played a significant role in driving reform" (p.5). The focus of the CAP has switched decisively from indiscriminate support of market prices to direct support of farm incomes and enhancement of the environment: Europe's butter mountains and wine lakes have long since disappeared. The practice of dumping agricultural products on world markets ended with the

---

* Section contributed by Graham Avery.

progressive reduction of export refunds from 1993 to practically zero by 2010. The reform process has had several major episodes, starting with the MacSharry reforms from 1992, which cut back on market support measures in exchange for income support. In 1999 market intervention prices were reduced and brought closer to world market prices, and from 2006 income support was decoupled from production levels.

The report on agriculture, like other reports, includes no explicit conclusions and makes no proposals. It explains scrupulously that it does not predetermine or prejudge proposals in the future for changes to the EU or about the appropriate balance of competences.

The first question addressed is "Should decisions on agricultural policy be made at the European, national, or other levels?" On this, the conclusions to be drawn from the Review are rather clear. In view of the single market for agricultural goods, and the EU's role in international negotiations on agricultural trade, the EU's competence in agricultural policy is justified. On the question of external competence, the evidence of the Scotch Whisky Association is particularly robust: it has "identified over 450 tariff and non-tariff barriers affecting Scotch in more than 150 of its export markets outside the EU. Future export growth for Scotch Whisky is therefore heavily dependent on the removal of trade barriers through the trade policy and market access work of the Commission" (p. 51).

But in relation to other objectives of agricultural policy, such as income support for the farming community, rural development, and the supply of environmental goods, the question of competence is more debatable. The Review suggests that more account should be taken under the CAP of the principle of subsidiarity. It quotes the powerful argument of Harald Grethe (Professor at Hohenheim University) that "the economic nature of direct payments has changed fundamentally, from a production subsidy to a sectoral and personal income policy" and that "sectoral and personal income transfer policies are generally designed and financed at the Member State level, not at the EU level" (p.52).

In the same line of argument, the report suggests more flexibility for national and regional implementation of EU rules, observing that diverse regional situations exist within the UK itself (England, Scotland, Wales, and Northern Ireland) and that some competences are already devolved to regional governments. But it warns that more flexibility could lead to problems of unequal application: greater discretion for member states can lead farmers to suspect that 'the grass is greener on the other side'. It recalls that a fundamental aim of the policy is to ensure fair competition between farmers in different member states and to avoid a subsidy race; it remarks that this tension between the need for recognition of local circumstances ('one size cannot fit all') and the need for fair competition ('the level playing field') has been identified in many other balance of competences reviews.

On environmental aspects of the CAP), the report remarks that agri-environment schemes have been beneficial across Europe and provide a regime for conservation that might not otherwise exist. Positive arguments are offered by the Royal Society for the Protection of Birds (RSPB) - with more than 1 million members, Europe's largest voluntary environmental organisation. The RSPB says that shared natural resources such as biodiversity, air, carbon stores and water require a cross-border approach, and that EU competence for agriculture, land management and plant health is clearly justified because these resources require an international framework for environmental protection. It also argues that the EU can take a longer-term view, and that its competence for agriculture helps to shield environmental investment from changes in government, and political priorities at national level.

The second major question addressed is "What are the policy's advantages or disadvantages from the point of view of the UK's interests?" The budgetary cost of the CAP) has always been a focus of criticism in Britain. The report correctly remarks that "the UK contribution to EU expenditure on agriculture is complicated by the fact that it does not contribute to the CAP but to the overall EU budget; and its contribution is net of the UK abatement, sometimes called the rebate" (p.37). However the report also cautions that "this makes it difficult to estimate a net UK contribution to the CAP, but it also reports the more direct assessment that the rebate "has neutralised for UK taxpayers a major part of the CAP's net costs" (p.38).

An interesting aspect of the Review is its examination of the implications for the UK of radical options such as leaving the Common Agricultural Policy), or leaving the European Union altogether. Here a key question is the level of national agricultural support that would replace the CAP: most respondents argued that it would be lower, but others noted that outside the EU both Norway and Switzerland have higher levels of agricultural support than the EU.

A group of former British government officials (the Senior European Experts Group) suggested that with a return to separate national subsidies, there would be such a wide variation in the degrees of subsidy that a level playing field would be impossible; without EU action, there would either be a subsidy race between member states determined to protect their farmers, or a breakdown of the single market, or both.

Several respondents argued that if the UK left the EU and followed the 'Norway option' (membership of the EEA) it would not have to apply the CAP but would nevertheless have to follow most single market rules, with no vote or influence over shaping them. The National Farmers Union commented that this would be "hugely risky to farmers, leading to lower farm prices, loss of the UK's major export market, and reduced protection from imports produced to a lower standard" (p.79).

On the question of British influence on the CAP) today, the report relays the plaintive comment that "the low number of UK nationals within the Commission means that our knowledge of agricultural economics and perspective on trade and the role of the market is not influencing the formulation of EU policy" (p.59).

Assessment

The Review on Agriculture, although critical of the CAP, shows that the policy has developed in ways that successive British governments have advocated; that the EU's role in this sector is justified in relation to the internal market and external trade; that there are limits to the extent to which the subsidiarity principle can be applied in a sector such as agriculture; and that if Britain left the EU, it would still be directly affected by EU rules. This is a balanced and realistic approach, which will not be what British Eurosceptics expected.

For the future, although the CAP is likely to remain a focus of British criticism, we can expect its long-term development to respond to the dynamics of the EU's economic and political situation. The need to focus the European budget's limited resources on policies that promote growth and investment, the requirement to adapt agricultural policy mechanisms to diverse national and regional situations, and the logic of financing social income aids at the national level, will continue to drive reform of the CAP in a rational direction.

The evidence at a glance – agriculture

Competence justified for single market and external trade reasons

Policy severely criticised, but reforms since 1990s are in directions advocated by the UK

Shift from production to income support

No more butter mountains, wine lakes and dumping on foreign markets

Repatriation of farm income support has some minority advocates

---

2.5   Fisheries*

The European Union has an unhappy record in fisheries. For many years policy-makers, including European Commissioners for Fisheries, denounced the failure of the Common Fisheries Policy (CFP) to achieve its objectives: fish stocks and employment in fisheries have been in constant decline. For the British, the policy had an inauspicious origin: it was adopted in 1970 by the 'Six' just before opening membership negotiations with the UK, which has more fisheries resources than any other EU member state. Successive attempts at reform failed to grasp the nettle of conserving fish stocks in order to support a sustainable industry. It is hardly surprising that British governments have been critical of the EU's role in the management of fisheries policy, and British Eurosceptics have targeted the CFP as a candidate for 'repatriation' of powers from the EU to the national level.

---

* Section contributed by Graham Avery.

But as a result of the decisions on reform of the CFP taken in 2013, this negative picture has changed. These decisions, taken jointly by the Council of Ministers and the European Parliament, include fundamental changes:

- a ban on 'discards' of fish at sea, to take effect between 2015 and 2019

- a legally binding commitment to fish at sustainable levels to achieve 'maximum sustainable yield' by 2015 where possible, and by 2020 at latest

- decisions on annual quotas to be underpinned by scientific advice

- decentralised decision-making, with regionalisation of fisheries management consistent with the principle of subsidiarity.

The results of these reforms, which came into force only in January 2014, are yet to be seen, and their success will depend on effective implementation and rigorous enforcement throughout the EU. However, they were welcomed by the British government, and have been perceived by British commentators as a successful case of UK advocacy of EU reform, aided by enlightened support from the European Parliament.

Against this background, the British government's Balance of Competences report on fisheries is positive in tone, declaring that "the recent reforms, for which the UK Government pressed, are considered by many to have taken major steps to address the policy's fundamental problems." Many respondents "highlighted the opportunities presented by the new regionalisation process" and hoped that it would "end micromanagement, decentralise decision-making and allow more responsive fisheries management, yet still offer the benefits of central EU coordination" (p.26)."

Two questions are the focus of the report, first the balance of competences between the EU and the UK, and then the more general question of how the EU affects the UK and its national interests.

The first question addressed is "Should decisions on fisheries policy be made at the European, national, or other levels?" On this, the report states that the majority of respondents support some form of supranational management of fisheries, due to the trans-boundary nature of fish stocks. Many respondents considered it essential to have a central coordinator to set conservation objectives for all countries with an interest in a particular fishery. It is not possible for one member state to achieve sustainable fisheries if another continues unsustainable practices, and conservation decisions at the EU level provide the opportunity to raise standards for fisheries management over a wider geographic area than the UK acting alone.

Many criticisms are made of the way in which decisions have been taken by the EU on the setting of catch limits, with annual negotiations leading to unsatisfactory political compromises. Here the government's report prudently refrains from comment, since British ministers took part in those political decisions. Concerning the quota system, the prize for candour goes to the Cornish Fish Producers Organisation, which states that although the system has many problems "it is very far from clear if any superior alternative is available."

A small number of respondents suggested alternative models of competence. A Conservative Party Green Paper and a report by the Tax-Payers' Alliance on "What Powers David Cameron Would Need to Repatriate" suggested that fisheries policy should revert to exclusive national control of fisheries resources. The United Kingdom Independence Party (UKIP) claimed that this would be worth £2.5bn per year to the British economy.

But others questioned whether these benefits could be achievable, given the shared nature of fisheries and the reduced strength of the UK's negotiating position. A group of former British government officials (Senior European Experts Group) argued that if competence for fisheries is repatriated, the UK would need to negotiate with other countries (including EU countries) who currently share access to stocks, and that it could not mount a credible case for an increase in quotas at the expense of other countries, given that the current shares have been unchanged for over 30 years and are themselves based on historical fishing activity.

The second question addressed is "What are the policy's advantages or disadvantages from the point of view of the UK's interests?" On the economic and social consequences of the CFP)," the report notes the decreasing numbers of vessels and fishermen in the UK, in line with the trends seen across the EU, although the extent to which this reflects more effective fishing techniques and technology is unclear. However, other evidence suggests that the declining trend preceded the UK's accession to the EU and was a global phenomenon; countries outside of the CFP had also seen similar declines in vessel numbers.

An interesting aspect of the report is its review of the implications of EU competence for reciprocal fisheries agreements with non-EU countries. Respondents pointed out that EU fisheries agreements with Norway and the Faroe Islands have delivered benefits for the UK. Thus British fishing opportunities in Norwegian waters are currently 'paid for' mostly by transfers of fishing opportunities from other member states to Norway. The report itself comments that the UK could reap benefits in the region of £17m. per annum from the Norway Agreement.

Assessment

The Review contains many justified criticisms of the Common Fisheries Policy, but is positive about the EU's recent decisions on reform. It is instructive in showing that, in British fisheries circles, the logic of EU competence and EU coordination is generally accepted. The European fisheries industry now has the prospect of a period of policy stability in which the various elements of the reform can be applied, and hopefully achieve the desired results.

The report also demonstrates that, in this sector, reform of a common policy has been successfully advocated and negotiated by the British government with its EU partners, with the aid of the European Parliament. This has wider implications for the British political debate on the EU. Statements of ministers quoted in the report are much more positive than what we usually hear from the British government.

According to the Deputy Prime Minister, Nick Clegg, "for years people said the Common Fisheries Policy was beyond reform. Yet we led the way on a historic agreement that will transform fishing practices across Europe, and end micro-management from Brussels, massively benefiting our fishing industry and our marine environment" (p.26). The Minister for

Europe, David Lidington, declares "this has shown how the UK can work successfully with European partners to deliver significant reforms that benefit our country" (p.26). These are political messages that, in the British context, should have a wider resonance.

The evidence at a glance – fisheries

Competence justified to prevent unsustainable over-fishing and external negotiations

Early policy severely criticised, but repatriation would be highly problematic

Radically reformed in 2013, with ban on discards at sea, binding sustainability constraints and more decentralised management

---

2.6 Food safety and animal welfare

There is a large amount of very detailed EU regulation here, and the Review lists almost one hundred regulations or directives. The summary conclusion of the Review was: "While many respondents expressed support for the current balance, the evidence also demonstrated several areas for improvement" (p.56). Respondents from the farm industry and related civil society organisations considered a harmonised approach to food safety and animal health as essential, and a competence for animal welfare at the EU level as "vital". The Consumer Advisory Panel of the UK Food Safety Agency felt that the UK benefits from being part of EU food law, with no rationale for operating alone. It was thought unlikely that national legislation by the UK would be less rigorous than current EU practice.

The UK's trade in food and beverages with the EU is twice that with the rest of the world. The industry is now structured with extensive cross-border supply chains across the EU, which could not function without common technical standards and/or mutual recognition. Moreover, for food safety these supply chains must observe strict hygiene controls.

Since 2003 the EU has been developing a far-reaching reform of its food law to tackle the problems of complex supply chains, establishing traceability obligations from covering 'farm to fork'. The horse-meat scandal of 2013, which reverberated around the EU, demonstrated the need for correct enforcement of EU regulations, and not a lightening repatriation of EU competence. This case illustrated a broader political point; that while there is much political rhetoric about over-regulation by Brussels, whenever a serious problem arises in the area of food safety the call is invariably to strengthen EU rules and/or their implementation.

The outbreak of so-called 'mad cow disease' (BSE) has been the most serious instance of a food safety problem of European and international concern originating in the UK, resulting in widespread banning of UK beef exports. When the problem was overcome EU legislation enforced the re-opening of EU markets in 2006, with the aid of a European Court of Justice to make a dissenting member state comply. Russia's ban lasted six years longer, however, while US and Japan markets remained closed.

Respondents for Scottish whisky interests and producers of regionally branded products noted the strength of EU branding protection both within the EU and in international markets.

The issue of whether the EU over-regulates or imposes excessive implementation burdens is discussed in the Review. The UK has been in the lead in advocating that the Commission progress with better and now smart regulation, with impact assessments needed to accompany all proposals. The Commission has been responding with new impact assessment guidelines, and annual publication of a report on application of the principles of subsidiarity and proportionality.[16] Key concepts are 'risk assessment' and 'risk management', given that regulations that seek to be too absolute in eliminating food safety problems will lead to unduly heavy burdens. EU food law recognises these concepts, but some respondents argued that the EU (and the European Parliament in particular) was at times inclined to be

---

[16] The Commission produces an annual report on subsidiarity and proportionality, of which the latest for 2012 was published in July 2013 at: http://eur-lex.europa.eu/LexUriServ/ LexUriServ.do?uri=COM:2013:0566:FIN:EN:PDF

unduly prescriptive and embrace proposals insufficiently based on scientific evidence. Important instances here involve highly controversial cases such as cloning and GMO elements in the food chain.

The olive oil packaging affair of 2013, already described in section 1.6 above) has become an iconic case of a proposed regulation that failed to take the subsidiarity principle seriously. While the Commission was at fault for embracing the proposal, its response to the public outcry in rapid withdrawal of the proposal illustrates the checks and balances that now exist around issue of subsidiarity.

Animal welfare respondents indicated the importance of the UK having influenced the shaping of EU standards in a progressive direction. This brings out an interesting aspect of defining 'British interests'. In this case the objective is to develop norms of significance for animal welfare as widely as possible, i.e. chickens in cages in general, not just 'British chickens'. While progress on this account worldwide is extremely difficult to secure, at the EU level the UK's leading advocacy has had a real impact.

Assessment

One of the most striking points made by the Review is that only 20% of consumers were aware that the EU was largely responsible for food safety regulation, while 75% preferred that it be a UK responsibility. This implies that the UK could do perfectly well by going it alone.

The evidence presented is the opposite on both accounts. The EU is largely responsible for food safety and animal welfare law, and the prospects of a seceding UK going it alone would pose huge problems, disrupting now well-established industrial networks and trading structures, without any apparent case for either raising or lowering standards. For these reasons respondents broadly endorsed the present attribution of competences to the EU.

The UK has been one of the most progressive influences within the EU on two accounts, first the case for 'smart' risk-contingent regulation, and second, for animal welfare.

Under the secession hypothesis it seems most probable that the UK would choose to keep EU standards on its books, at least initially. But if it then chose not to follow new EU legislation and to innovate with its own, there would be the perennial question of whether this would prejudice access to the single market.

The food safety and animal welfare sector illustrates the huge disconnect between, on the one hand, professionally informed opinion in the UK, and on the other hand the present state of public opinion, and indeed the hazards of resolving this difference by an 'in-or-out' referendum vote.

The evidence at a glance – food safety and animal welfare

Agri-food industry considers harmonised EU approach essential

No rationale for national competence

UK regulations would not be less rigorous

Since 2003 far-reaching reform establishing 'traceability' in the food chain

Scotch whisky sector values protection of branding in EU and world markets

UK advocates smart regulation, with risk assessment methodology

UK plays leading role in shaping EU animal welfare standards

2.7 Public health

Although public health is a relatively new EU competence at the level of treaty provisions, standards for products involved in public health care have long been subject to EU legislation under its single market competence (medicines, medical devices, organs, nutrition and labelling, tobacco and alcohol, etc.). In addition, there are important EU legislation implications for public health policies in the area of free movement of persons, the provision of services, and employment policy. While these activities are of considerable importance, the treaties nonetheless make it clear that the competence for organising and delivering health care lies with the member states.

This Review is notably rich in content and in the contributions by professional stakeholders, including medical and nursing professions and industries supplying medicines and medical devices. Overall, on the basis of evidence submitted, it was observed that stakeholders considered the present balance of competences to be "broadly appropriate" (p.8).

For medicines and medical devices, the majority of respondents felt that the balance of competences was right. "The EU helps ensure a high standard of health safety across the EU, early launch in the UK of new medicines and medical technologies, and the competitiveness of the UK life sciences industry" (p.27).

The EU works on selected public health issues. EU directives now assure the free movement of blood, organs, tissues and cells, subject to minimum standards. This is recognised to be beneficial for patients. EU activity for nutrition and food labelling, which has been harmonised for over 30 years, is judged by respondents, including the government, to be appropriate, serving the UK well. As regards action over tobacco that stresses its harmful effects on health, most respondents felt the current balance of competences was working well. Similar views are expressed as regards alcohol, with harmful drinking a particular challenge in the UK.

The EU has established systems for the surveillance and early warning of communicable diseases. This is appreciated by respondents, including the government, as adding real value.

The impact of the Working Time Directive on the public health sector is a well-known subject of criticism from the UK. The Review makes a balanced assessment, noting the benefits that may be provided for the work-life balance of medical staff, and avoidance of treatment by tired staff. The main criticism is over the lack of flexibility in the directive to accommodate the needs of different operating environments, and in particular problems for the supply of continuous care, avoiding too much staff turnover.

The relevant EU directive assures recognition of professional qualifications, such that there are in general no restrictions on EU nationals to move within the EU labour market. This is of particular importance to the UK as a substantial net importer of health professionals. Gaps in skills within the UK can be rapidly filled. The nursing profession now relies heavily on nurses from other EU countries.

An EU directive clarifies the rights of citizens to purchase health care in 'other' EU countries and to claim reimbursement from their home country. The UK makes good use of this provision, with 400,000 British pensioners in Spain, for example.

The UK is the largest beneficiary of EU funding of health research under the Framework programmes, which are a significant driver of cross-border partnerships and information dissemination in the heath sector.

Assessment

The EU's competences in the public health sector consist of a portfolio of very specific activities, which do not impinge on the responsibilities of the member states to run their own health services. EU actions are clearly complementary to national competences, and address issues that cannot be easily or efficiently handled at the national level. There are some friction points with respect to details, and maybe most of all over the Working Time Directive, but these should not obscure the main message that the EU is adding value, and that the balance of competences is judged to be broadly appropriate.

The Review reveals quite a number of specific fields in which the UK clearly benefits from EU activity, ranging from medical product standardisation to research. While UK public opinion decries excessive immigration in general, the National Health Service would be in much greater difficulty without the free movement of labour within the EU, given that it is a considerable net importer of health professionals.

The evidence at a glance – public health

Valuable niche competences judged broadly appropriate by stakeholders

Do not impinge on national competence for health services

Regulation by EU important for UK life sciences industries

Free movement of doctors and nurses fills gaps in skills

Cross-border health care system arrangements significant, e.g. for 400,000 British retired in Spain

---

2.8   Digital information rights

This is the most future-oriented of all the Reviews, and addresses the twin concerns of data protection and access to information in the digital era now associated with the rise of Big Data, Cloud Computing, and the Internet of Things (IoT). Action at EU and/or international level was generally argued by respondents to be needed for two reasons; first because data flows know no national borders, and secondly because of the need for common standards for business and consumers (p.6).

Data protection. The core legal basis for EU competence in the field of data protection lies in Article 16 (TFEU) of the Lisbon Treaty: "Everyone has the right to the protection of personal data concerning them". The text goes on to say that the EU should lay down the rules for this purpose as regards activities that fall within the scope of EU law and rules relating to the free movement of such data. The EU's key legislation in this field, the Data Protection Directive of 1995, was based on somewhat narrower earlier treaty provisions. This directive was in turn transposed into UK law with the Data Protection Act of 1998. The substantive provisions are about the rights of the individual to access data held by data processors about them, a right to object to such data being processed, to have such data rectified if inaccurate, or to be erased, and to claim compensation for breaches of such rights.

A key debate among respondents was over how to strike the right balance between harmonisation and flexibility, which in the EU's legal context focuses on the choice between the directive versus the regulation as an instrument of action; the former allows for greater flexibility but implies higher compliance costs for businesses operating in the 28 member states. The main point here is that the arguments are not about whether the EU should have a competence in this field or not – that debate has a clear conclusion, namely that EU action is required. The real issue is about striking the optimal balance between harmonisation versus degrees of freedom for individual member states to implement common rules in ways that suit national traditions or cultures.

Many respondents felt that "the current Directive struck a good balance between the interests of data controllers and citizens. .... However, almost all respondents felt that the Directive has not kept pace with technological changes. This is particularly relevant in the light of complex developments such as cloud computing" (p.3). This question of balance is also one of the rights of individuals versus the objective of promoting economic growth with advanced digital technologies, which many respondents felt to be well satisfied (p.29).

A further debate concerns the balance between EU versus international action, and here many respondents argued that the EU was well positioned to develop common rules and thence to promote its standards globally (p.50). While a global regime would be impossible to enforce, the EU was much better placed than individual member states to influence the shaping of important global trends, notably through ongoing negotiations with the US in the TTIP framework, and potentially through cooperation with Asian-Pacific countries in the APEC framework.

The European Court of Justice has been active in various cases over some of the finer but still major issues of interpretation of the law. For example, in 2014 the CJEU ruled in a case referred to it by the Spanish data protection agency where an individual wanted the *Google* search engine to delete personal information about him. In May 2014 the Court found against *Google*, even in an instance where the data processing of the search engine was performed outside the EU. The case became known as being about 'the right to be forgotten'. There followed in November 2014 (too late to be referred to in the Review) a decision by the European Commission's competition authority to open an antitrust investigation into allegations that *Google Inc.* had abused a dominant position in online search, in violation of European Union rules (Article 102 TFEU).

The Review goes into some detail about the future challenges for the data protection regulator posed by three inter-related digital phenomena: 'big data', i.e. very large data sets characterised by the '3 Vs' – volume, variety and velocity combined with the frequent use of algorithms. This includes such phenomena as cloud computing, which involves ubiquitous network access to powerful computing resources, and 'the internet of things', which encompasses the IT content of virtually all goods and services such as phones, medical devices, smart home appliances, banking services, cars etc.

The Review highlights the UK's keen interest in being a world leader in these technologies.

It goes on to discuss the complex data protection issues that rapidly emerge alongside the spectacular growth of the digital economy under these various headings. Revision and updating of the EU's regulatory framework is currently work in progress with negotiations over Commission proposals, published in January 2012, for a comprehensive new Data Protection Regulation to replace the existing 1995 Directive. There is also a proposal for a new directive on police and judicial cooperation aspects.

The Review reports the UK government view that the most suitable instrument of EU action is the directive rather than a regulation, on the grounds that the former allows for more flexibility to take into account varying national cultures and legal practices. However, the debate among independent respondents was more nuanced, with harmonisation through a regulation offering advantages of legal clarity and economy for implementation across the 28 member states.

Access to information. The EU has established its own freedom of information act. This was first set out in the Amsterdam Treaty of 1995, and carried over in Article 15 (TFEU) of the Lisbon Treaty, which states that "Any citizens of the Union, and any natural or legal person residing in or having its registered office in a Member State, shall have the right of access to documents of the Union institutions, bodies, offices and agencies, whatever their medium....". The detailed rules for implementing these treaty provisions have been established in the Public Access to Documents Regulation (1049/2011).

Respondents "from a broad range of sectors highlighted the positive impact of the … Regulation to the extent that it increases the transparency of EU policy-making" (p.44), although it was reported to be often difficult to obtain documents through this regulation. On the other hand, some respondents reported that access to EU documents allowed them to influence EU policy before it became legislation. Many respondents felt there was no need to change EU competence in this field, or to reduce or augment it.

Assessment

The data protection agenda has acquired hugely increased importance as a function of the spectacular growth of the digital economy. The Review is essentially about how to regulate this increasingly complex technological environment at the EU level, since the need for EU competence in this field was not contested. The real issues are about how best to regulate, with the choice of legal mode being between directive versus regulation for the new EU legislation. This approximates to choice being between more or less strictly harmonised approaches. Negotiations are ongoing for a proposed EU law on this matter.

The EU's own 'freedom of information act' proves to be a rather simple affair. It was welcomed on grounds of improving transparency of EU policy-making, with no pressures for changing the EU's competence here.

Various respondents pointed out that in the hypothesis of secession the UK would still need in practice to comply with EU data protection requirements.

The evidence at a glance – information rights

Data protection as a matter of EU competence is uncontested.

The issues concern:

... how strictly harmonised EU law should be (including the directive v. regulation question)

... how regulatory policy should best cope with the rapid pace of technological change

... how the EU can best influence emerging global standards

The regulation on public access to EU documents is broadly positive, favouring transparency in EU policy-making

---

3.   Economic, monetary and social policies

3.1   *Economic and monetary union**

This Review surveys the macroeconomic policy landscape of the EU, and in particular that of the eurozone, in considerable detail. Given the seriousness of the problems of the eurozone, but also the UK's detachment from it, we choose to tackle head-on the outstanding issues, more than is sometimes the case in the Review.

Macroeconomic policy coordination mechanisms. The Review provides a detailed account of the mechanisms of macroeconomic policy coordination within the EU as a whole, and of the eurozone in particular. The treaty provisions on economic and monetary policy apply in principle to all member states that have signed up to treat economic policy as a common concern. In reality, however, only members of the euro area have subjected themselves to binding provisions. The UK government thus remains completely free to set its own monetary and fiscal policies.

The Review affirms the UK's interest in seeing a successful and dynamic eurozone, but underlines that this will require systemic reforms with closer economic and fiscal integration for its members. It would seem that the current system of economic policy coordination does not work properly, or in the more polite language of the Review, "ha[s] not always been effective" (p.2). In particular, this applies to the coercive elements that concern only the eurozone in the Stability Pact, the Fiscal Compact and the Macroeconomic Imbalances Procedure. The Stability Pact with its (in)famous limit on deficits of 3% of GDP has been in force since the start of EMU. But its *modus operandi* has changed several times; and when 'push came to shove' with Germany and France in 2003-04 it was in effect put into abeyance by a majority in the Council. The latest revision of the Stability Pact introduced under the so-called 'Six Pack' was supposed to make it 'smarter' by emphasising deficits adjusted for the economic cycle or the output gap. However, the dispute over the calculation of the output gap for Italy in 2014 showed that this change only made it more

---

* Section contributed by Daniel Gros.

difficult to enforce a continuing fiscal adjustment in weak economies because the governments of the countries with poor growth put forward the argument that the Commission had not chosen the proper method for calculating the cyclical adjustment.

The inverse majority rule that was introduced under the so-called Six Pack was supposed to give the Commission a stronger position in enforcing the Stability Pact requirements, given that member countries are unlikely to vote for sanctions on their peers, fearing that next time around they might be on the receiving end. However, the way in which the Commission acquiesced to the arguments of France and Italy in late 2014 that their fiscal adjustments should be considered satisfactory, although arguably in both cases they were incompatible with their previous commitments, shows that the Commission did not dare to use the formal power it had been given. The decision to accept the Italian and French budget proposals was essentially taken by the President of the Commission, overriding the opinions of the technical staff in the competent DG ECFIN. The coercive part of the Stability Pact has thus *de facto* again been put aside.

The Fiscal Compact, which introduces a requirement for lowering the debt ratio, is as yet untested, but its application would appear to be challenging in an environment characterised by slow growth and deflation, which makes a reduction in the debt ratio extremely difficult. The underlying assumption under the numerical rule of the Fiscal Compact (a reduction in the debt/GDP ratio to reduce the excess of the actual debt/GDP ratio over 60% by 1/20 per year) was that nominal GDP would grow by 5% per annum.

The Macroeconomic Imbalances Procedure (MIP) was introduced after the 2008 crisis to prevent the recurrence of a boom like that in Spain or Ireland. However, no such boom with rapid domestic demand growth and large current account deficits is expected for the time being, and the MIP has so far been applied in an asymmetric manner. Countries with current account surpluses above the norm of 6% (like the Netherlands or Germany) have not been asked to adjust policies.

Overall, the coercive elements in the eurozone's system of coordination have not *de facto* been used effectively, except when combined with conditional macro-financial assistance.

Systemic reform of the eurozone. While the reforms to the eurozone's economic governance framework appear to have been ineffective so far, the response to the crisis has produced two key institutional innovations, which have been or promise to be, very effective and important.

The first innovation was the creation of a permanent rescue fund, the European Stability Mechanism (ESM), which operates outside the treaty framework, but has been instrumental in providing financing for the adjustment in five (counting Spain with its limited support for the banking sector) countries. In four cases the adjustment has been successful in the sense that the recipient countries have been able to exit the programme with a resumption of market access, a recovery in the economy and an improvement in the fiscal balances and the current account. Greece constitutes the only case where the problems continue (on which more below).

The second institutional innovation in reaction to the crisis is the complex phenomenon named Banking Union. A key element here is the shift of the responsibility for the supervision of the largest 120+ banks to the ECB, which has become the direct supervisor of the bulk of the euro area's banking system since November of 2014. Another element is the gradual creation of a common 'Single Resolution Fund' (SRF) to finance the resolution of failing banks (i.e. a fund to prevent a repetition of the disorderly Lehman insolvency). There has been much debate about the adequacy of its size and the absence of a fiscal backstop. All one can say at this point is that by about 2020 the SRF, which will be four- to five-times larger than the corresponding UK fund, will be strong enough to deal with problems at any one of even the largest euro area banks, or with problems of the entire banking system of a small- to medium-sized country.

The Banking Union is, however, incomplete in the sense that there is no common fund for deposit insurance. But the two elements that have been put in place should make the eurozone much more resilient to national financial shocks. The 'Balkanisation' of the eurozone's banking markets, which was observed in 2011-13, should thus not be repeated in future. The combination of the ESM plus the two elements of the Banking Union represent the key innovations that should allow the euro area to deal with future shocks, both from irresponsible governments and regional financial market disruptions.

Postscript

Prospects for macroeconomic recovery of the eurozone. The Review largely abstains from the currently vital question of whether or when the eurozone might finally return to a sustained recovery. At the time of writing, January 2015, this may have become likely at last, not so much because of adequate economic policies, but because of two favourable external shocks, namely the depreciation of the euro against the dollar and the steep fall in the oil price. However, the latter is likely to reinforce the deflationary tendencies anyway latent in the euro area where internal demand remains structurally weak. The deflationary impact of the oil price is likely to be stronger than the slightly inflationary impulse resulting from the depreciation of the euro against the dollar, mainly because the effective exchange rate of the euro has moved very little since most trading partners of the euro area have also depreciated against the dollar. The ECB so far seems to have been losing the fight to reach its inflation target of 2%, leading to the debate about whether or what kind of quantitative easing (QE) should be introduced. The issue here is how far the bank-based structure of the euro area's financial system makes the prime weapon against deflation, namely QE, less effective. However, at the end of January 2015 the ECB did announce a substantial programme of asset purchases. The intention is to buy 60 billion euro worth of assets each month until the end of 2016, of which about 50 billion are likely to be government bonds. The ECB also announced that the asset purchases could continue if the path of inflation had not converged, by the end of the schedule of asset purchases, towards the ECB's goal of below, but close to 2%. Another contributing factor to the recovery of the euro area has been the surprise decision of the Swiss National Bank to end the policy of defending a lower bound for the Swiss franc exchange rate against the euro. The immediate appreciation of the Swiss franc led to a fall in the effective exchange rate of the euro of almost 2%.

The continuing Greek crisis. The Review makes only a passing reference to events in Greece, and deserves further comment.

Greece has distinguished itself by the slow and unwilling implementation of reforms since the start of its adjustment programme, which had to be changed regularly, with five reviews by 2014. The snap elections of January 2015 led to a new government dominated by Syriza, which had consistently campaigned against austerity and the adjustment programme imposed, in their eyes, by the Troika. Given the explicit request of the new government for debt relief and the renewed large-scale deposit withdrawals, concerns have resurfaced about Greece possibly leaving the euro area., Opinion polls have consistently revealed that 60% of the Greek population wishes to keep the euro, however, and most political parties agree on this. At the same time, a large part of the Greek population seems to support the request to reduce the debt burden for the country and to end austerity. These demands appear to be in stark contrast to the obligations that Greece undertook under the adjustment programme. A typical 'euro-fudge' might solve this apparent contradiction through a limited rescheduling of some official debt payments, combined with a relaxation of the fiscal targets. In the end, the difference between governments that have never implemented promises to pay and a new government that promises not to pay might not be that great. It is, of course, possible that a bank run sets in if clashes between the Greek authorities and Brussels and Berlin become too heated. However, even if Greek depositors were to panic, an exit from the eurozone is not inevitable, as the experience of Cyprus shows. The solution might then consist of some capital controls to pretend that Greece is still part of the eurozone. The Greek problem might thus be contained, at least in the short run.

Assessment

The UK's opt-out, not only from the eurozone's monetary regime, but also from the coercive elements of its fiscal policy coordination arrangements, mean that it stands aside from the difficult ongoing task of reforming the eurozone system. The Review noted some blurring of competences for the eurozone between the EU institutions and member states, but while justified this does not concern the UK.

It is difficult to determine how far the UK may have benefited from not joining the euro area. Recent growth figures show the UK as emerging much more quickly from the Great Financial Crisis than eurozone members. But if one looks at a longer time period the picture is not so clear. The chart below shows the UK GDP per capita at PPP relative to that of the eurozone from the early 1990s, when the UK did better than the continent, probably because it benefited from the boom in global finance. When the financial crisis occurred the UK initially suffered more, but more recently it has partly caught up again. It remains to be seen whether the better performance over the last few years represents just a temporary phenomenon, or a more permanent advantage for the UK, for example if the eurozone were to be inherently condemned to deflation and secular stagnation.

The present divergence in the external positions of the UK and the euro area is also very striking. The UK has run a current-account deficit for over a decade now and even the substantial devaluations of the pound against the euro after 2008 have not changed this. Exchange rate flexibility has thus apparently had little impact on the external balance of the UK, which has continued to deteriorate with a current-account deficit rising to around 4% of GDP, while the eurozone's surplus has continued to continued to deteriorate with a current account deficit rising to around 4% of GDP, while the eurozone's surplus continued to improve to over €200 billion, or close to 2.5% of the euro area's GDP. The UK, with its continuing current-account deficit and thus an ever-increasing foreign debt, will naturally choose different policy priorities from the eurozone, with its large surplus. A question not discussed in the Review is whether this UK external deficit is storing up a problem for the future.

The Review concludes with a summary of the risks for the UK of the eurozone moving increasingly towards 'caucusing' on macroeconomic policy and on financial market matters, leading to discriminatory treatment of British interests (p.99). The Review stresses the need for vigilance on this point, but might more clearly have drawn the conclusion that to minimise these risks the UK needs to position itself as a constructive member state, whereas the secession scenario would only maximise these risks.

The evidence at a glance – economic and monetary policy

UK has opt-out for both eurozone and coercive aspects of fiscal policy coordination

Coercive rules for eurozone fiscal policy, aside from conditional financial assistance, have proved ineffective

Systemic reforms of eurozone (funding mechanisms and Banking Union) are more effective

Eurozone macroeconomic recovery now more likely, due to the oil shock, plus new quantitative easing measures

UK benefits from earlier economic recovery, but longer term prospects are not so clear

UK concerns over discriminatory 'caucusing' by eurozone members not evident so far

Figure 1. UK economic performance relative to the eurozone, 1993-2016

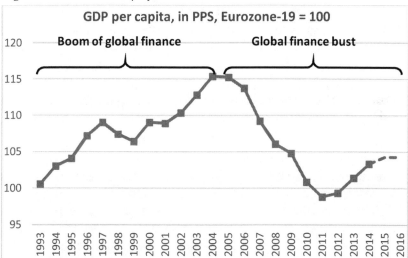

Source: D. Gros and M. Busse, own calculations.

3.2 Social and employment policy*

This review of a notoriously controversial field of EU competence – social and employment policy – starts with a chronological map of its development. In the beginning, social and employment policy did not have its own legal base. When social objectives were pursued, it was always with reference to the economic union, i.e. they were issues that were covered to the extent that they related to the primary goal of the union, which was the sound functioning of the common market. The 1992 Maastricht Treaty was the first to recognise social and employment policy as an objective worthy of pursuit not merely with regard to its relation to the common market, but as a goal in itself. The Social Chapter of the Maastricht Treaty, which broadened the EU competence in the field of social policy legislation, met with strong opposition from the UK Conservative government, which secured an opt-out provision for itself. The UK came to be bound by the Social Chapter only in 1997, as a result of its Labour government's agreement to accede to it as part of the Treaty of Amsterdam.

Discussion of the development of the EU competence within the social and employment policy ends with the conclusion that the 2009 Lisbon Treaty ultimately broadened the scope of EU competences by adding the "well-being of its people" to the objectives of the Union, and fully acknowledging the importance of the pursuit of social justice and social progress. Furthermore, it stresses the combat against social discrimination and inequalities.

Before the Review moves to the views of the respondents, it introduces the main articles in the EU treaties that serve as a basis for the directives and regulations in social and employment policy. It frames the competence the EU has within those fields as the "competence to adopt measures in health and safety at work, conditions of work and social security, and competence to ensure cooperation between Member States". With regard to this range of competences, it is interesting to note that while the UK frequently resisted adoption of the pertinent EU legislation, in many cases the UK's own pre-existing legislation was already adhering to these

---

* Section contributed by Miroslav Beblavý and Alzbeta Hájková.

principles. The illustration of such a case used by the Review is a Health and Safety at Work Act (1974), which in fact inspired the European directive on measures to encourage improvements in the safety and health of workers, although the directive was more prescriptive in its nature than the original act.

The next part of the Review, dealing with results of the public consultation, confirms that this area of EU policy is highly controversial, and respondents' views range from the uncompromisingly negative to the resoundingly positive and offer no clear median. Interestingly, the previously discussed link between the EU as a primarily economic union and the EU as a community that ought to promote social progress was also explored by the respondents. Many argue that setting minimum requirements in the social policy area guarantees that businesses and workers within the single market have the same basic level of protection. On the other hand, various business respondents considered EU-level social and employment policy to be a burden, and were convinced that their business would benefit if EU regulations were lifted.

Upon being called to assess the role of social partners, respondents were not negative in principle about their role in the defining of market rules as such. Rather, they expressed worries that certain types of business and workers (e.g. small or micro businesses, and part-time workers) are often disenfranchised, which decreases the overall representativeness of the negotiations.

The Review makes it clear that the feedback from the respondents was quite negative when it came to adoption of minimum requirements. The general view is that the EU often goes beyond what would be a proper EU-wide minimum in the realm of health and safety at work issues, and imposes higher standards than are necessary. These standards are, in the opinion of many respondents, excessively prescriptive, opaque, and disproportionate with regard to the different economies of individual member states. In addition, they often represent additional costs for businesses. The Working Time and Temporary Agency Workers Directives are the ones that were marked as the costliest, with a negative impact on business.

Respondents also felt that when it comes to implementation of the EU directives, the UK is particularly careful about applying

the legislation 'to the letter'. The Review claims that there is a
commonly held belief in the UK that it is more thorough in
enforcing the EU legislation than other member states, which
supposedly puts it at a disadvantage, precisely because EU
legislation is perceived as something burdensome. The Review
also notes that this sentiment is generally not supported by
evidence.

The European Court of Justice is also seen as an element that
is harmful to national interests in its interpretation of the EU laws
in the fields of employment and discrimination. On the other
hand, the Review makes an important observation that the Court
tends to side with individuals, hence giving them a chance to have
a full reliance on and take advantage of the rights guaranteed by
the EU law. It is precisely individuals that, according to the
Review, profit the most from EU social and employment rules.
While businesses might perceive many aspects of EU policy as
burdensome, a number of respondents indicated that the same
policy contributed to creating a better work environment in terms
of equal pay, anti-discrimination, the status of part-time workers,
worker protection and health and safety at work. Another notable
positive point made is that as a whole, EU law is more stable than
national law and hence provides a solid basis for a business to plan
its future.

Assessment

Three major conclusions emerge from the Review. First, while
there are many anecdotes and case studies available, claims about
either the positive or negative effects of EU competences in social
and employment policy on the British economy or its workers are
hardly ever supported by quantitative evidence. This often means
that partisans resort to arguments based on 'first principles'. The
Review was not intended to and could not, produce original
datasets or evidence to remedy this.

Secondly, a small number of regulations appear to account
for much of the controversy. It is obvious from the text that the
directives on working time and agency workers are where EU
legislation causes many stakeholders discomfort, or, at the very
least, much irritation. Any renegotiation of the UK's relationship

with the EU in social and employment policy would likely focus on this area.

Thirdly, the British self-image of exceptionalism both does and does not match reality. The Review demonstrated two types of British exceptionalism – one real and one probably fictional. The first is in how employment is organised in the UK compared to most continental countries – being less focused as it is on full-time work and the traditional employer-employee relationship. The second is the perception, which can probably also be found in a number of member states, that "others do much less implementation and enforcement than 'we' do".

The evidence at a glance – social and employment policies

Strong support for 'social Europe' competence in much of EU

Contested in the UK, but divergences in political parties and interest groups

History of UK policy zig-zags, with opt-out of Social Chapter in 1992, opt-back-in in 1997, and current pressures for selective opt-outs

Loudest UK complaints over small number of regulations (working time and agency workers)

3.3 Cohesion policy*

This Review examines the objectives of the EU's cohesion policy, its performance, the impacts within the EU, and the potential costs and benefits for the UK in the development of regions. Given the large number of objectives and measures covered by the policy policies, its evaluation is complex. The policy comprises a number of instruments with different territorial dimensions and objectives, namely the Structural Funds, composed of the European Regional Development Fund (ERDF), the European Social Fund (ESF), the Cohesion Fund, the Connecting Europe Facility (formerly the Trans-European networks), the European Solidarity Fund and the European Aid to the Most Deprived Persons.

---

* Section contributed by Jorge Núñez Ferrer.

The main objective has always been balanced territorial development across the EU, but over the years it has become something of a tool to achieve a multiplicity of other EU objectives, such as those for sustainable growth, energy and climate change, with contributions to industrial policy and the completion of the single market. As a result, all regions in the EU are now eligible for funding from cohesion policy, albeit with different intensities.

The Review starts with an historical account of the development of the policy and the latest reforms undertaken for the Multiannual Financial Framework 2014-2020 and follows with a review of evidence on its rationale and performance.

The report has to contend with the lack of clear evidence in favour or against the cohesion policy. There are a large number of position papers either defending or condemning the policy, but studies with solid results on the impact of the policy are inconclusive, principally because the financial size of the cohesion policy is small compared to the EU GDP and that of most member states. There is, however, evidence that in some areas the policy is important for recipient regions. However, this does not solve the problem of the right distribution of competences and it is left to the reader to reach a conclusion.

For the Review the following questions were at the core of the analysis:

- Should the EU have a cohesion policy, in particular with regional redistributive aspects, or should redistribution be entirely a national competence?
- Should the EU be financing programmes in rich member states, in particular those that are not for cross-border objectives?
- Are the programmes yielding value for money?
- Are the management of funds and administrative requirements reasonable and proportional to the level of EU support?

For poorer member states there seems to be a general consensus that the cohesion policy is a good thing. Only a minority of the views submitted defends the thesis that the policy should be focusing more strictly on promoting economic growth, given that the returns on investment tend to be higher in the most developed regions. The policy should thus be reformed to focus on growth poles. The prevailing view was that the solidarity principle at EU level should be supported. Solidly researched counterfactual analysis comparing the situation to one without the support has not proved feasible, however.

The second question is the core issue in the report, with a considerable number of experts giving evidence favouring the elimination of support to richer countries, even if most support the distributive role for the poorest member states. The central argument presented is simply the circular nature of the financial flows. The money spent in the UK seems to correspond to the contribution of the beneficiary regions to the EU budget in this policy area. The argument goes that the money could have been spent directly in the regions without the costs and burden of sending it through Brussels. Estimates show that the average contribution of the beneficiary regions to the cohesion policy through the UK budget contribution is nearly identical to the amount they receive in return.

In the negotiations the British government used this argument in negotiations over the Multiannual Financial Framework for 2014-2020, namely the challenge to the notion that cohesion policy should also be spent in richer member states. Should the EU have a redistributive role from richer to poorer regions within richer countries? This depends on the interpretation of the main objectives of the policy. According to the Commission, the EU budget also has an important allocative role, not only a redistributive one. It is designed to promote EU priorities that would not be pursued separately by member states, or would be less efficient. National programmes would not replace EU ones, but would pursue objectives influenced by potentially narrower local priorities that risk being less valuable in the longer term and lead to lower growth in the EU as a whole. It also severs the cohesion policy's links with the EU's industrial policy.

The Review finds little evidence of the superiority of a policy administered through Brussels from one run domestically. However, the local government authorities of the UK are strong defenders of the cohesion policy programmes. The Welsh government argued that the strong redistributive nature of EU regional policy was necessary, given the absence of a robust national regional policy. There is a reasonable doubt expressed by local authorities whether, if the cohesion policy ended, London would spend the money saved to support the lagging regions to the same extent. Another argument favouring EU operations in the regions is the multiannual structure of the policy, allowing programmes to be protected from national annual budgetary cycles and thus offering stability. Some experts point to benefits of having a coordinated policy approach across the EU through the benefits of best-practice exchange.

Regarding value for money, the report considers that the evidence is inconclusive for the policy as a whole, but there is some evidence that the UK benefits from EU policies targeting the development of the single market, in particular for cross-border networks and from economic improvements in poorer member states. For other investments the report sees little benefit. It also asks whether some measures of the policy, particularly distributive policies of the European Social Fund, should be exclusively for national bodies. Some social policies have been introduced that the UK government considers to go beyond the remit of the cohesion policy.

Finally, there is a concern over the administrative burden of EU funding. The UK agrees that EU funding needs solid controls, but does question some of the measures in place. A particular mention has been placed for cumbersome auditing requirements in member states that have already well-established and functioning auditing structures.

Assessment

The Review does not present an explicit government position on the right balance of competences, and principally presents the evidence submitted by experts, regional authorities, administrators of the policy, parliamentarians and other interested parties. However, the concluding chapter on the way forward draws some careful final recommendations, which are very similar to existing positions of the UK government.

The main argument of the Review, from a balance of competences point of view, is the lack of rationale for the EU to spend cohesion policy resources in richer member states. It tends to support, in line with the existing position of the government, the ending of support to richer member states, with the exception of trans-European network projects and some limited specific programmes in favour of promoting competitiveness at EU level. The report does acknowledge that ending the funding to richer member states would require the agreement of all member states, and that this is unlikely. The report also indicates that the cohesion funds are strongly supported in Scotland, Wales and Northern Ireland. In the highly charged political climate surrounding and following the September 2014 referendum in Scotland, the evident sensitivity of proposals to scrap the cohesion funds in richer states deserves due understanding in London.

More plausibly, the UK could push for reform in the sense of procedural simplification. Some of the administrative requirements of the policy are excessive where member states have solid domestic institutions and control systems. It is possible that agreements could be reached on the accreditation of national auditing authorities and practices for such countries. It may also manage to convince the EU to allow for less bureaucratic but more results-oriented, risk-based approaches to auditing. On this the UK may be able to win the support of other member states.

The evidence at a glance – cohesion policy

Competence for a regional solidarity policy generally supported

UK advocates restriction to less rich member states, not accepted by all

Multiplicity of objectives (regional, energy, climate, industrial policy) makes evaluation difficult

Lack of clear evidence on impact on regional disparities

Procedural simplification advocated, in which well performing national auditing bodies are accredited to use their own controls

---

3.4 EU budget

The EU budget serves principally to support several specific policies, including agriculture, the structural funds, research and external relations, and these are reviewed in their respective sector reports, without being duplicated here. The present Review is therefore confined to cross-cutting issues raised by the budget.

Among the issues considered by the British government to be of the highest priority is the aggregate evolution of the budget, which currently amounts to €142 billion per year. The British government has worked hard this past year to restrain the growth of the budget, and claimed a major reform in securing the first ever reduction in real terms in the new Multiannual Financial Framework (MFF) for 2014-2020. The report notes the agreed real cut of 3.4% as an example of how the UK can work for reform of the EU through regular procedures, even qualifying this somewhat euphorically as an 'historic' achievement. Alongside important cuts being made in national budgets, the MFF saw the EU make commitments to reducing staff numbers in the institutions by 5%, and to increase the retirement age for EU civil servants from 65 to 66 years.

The report recognises that the budget is of a very modest size compared to that found in federal economic and monetary unions. There is debate about whether the eurozone should have its own budget of significant macroeconomic size, and if so whether this should become part of the EU budget. The UK Treasury has, from outside the eurozone, argued that this should be the case. While there is little political momentum in favour of such a development, it would in any case be irrelevant for the UK as it remains outside the eurozone.

The second issue highlighted is the distinction between what the report calls 'high EU-value added' expenditure versus low value added categories. Research and innovation, and expenditure under the heading 'connecting Europe' (transport infrastructures, energy networks) are placed in the high category, with agriculture in the low category, and the cohesion policy of the Structural Funds somewhere in between (see section 3.3 above). In fact, the proportions between the major blocks of spending have been very slowly undergoing significant change over the years in the direction of high value added policies. For example, in 1984 agriculture accounted for 66% of the budget. By 2014 it had declined to 40% and by 2020 it is planned to further decline to 34%. It is noted that the build-up of the structural funds started with the creation of the Regional Fund in the 1970s as an initiative promoted notably by the UK and Italy.

These changing expenditure structures are key to the debate around a third major issue, namely the British rebate, or 'abatement' in EU jargon, which returns to the UK a significant amount of its net contribution to the budget. The origin of the rebate goes back to the first British renegotiation of 1973-74, when the predominance of agricultural spending in the budget, and the relatively small size of the British farming sector, resulted in the UK paying the highest amount of net contributions per capita. This rebate (or 'corrective mechanism') has been enhanced and revised over time, while becoming more complicated as other big net payers also sought a degree of compensation. The Review shows that in 2012 the UK received the lowest amount of EU expenditure per capita of all member states, and that its net contribution to the budget before the rebate was correspondingly the highest; but after the rebate the UK's net contribution was the fifth largest and the middle of a core group of 'old' member states, including Germany, France, Italy, Sweden, Finland and the Netherlands.

The Review sets out the debate around whether the rebate is a good idea or not. Academics criticise it for distorting incentives between member states in their negotiations over policy-making, while recognising that it is a political response to an unbalanced expenditure structure. If this were corrected, then the rebate could be scrapped. The British government's view is that as long as the expenditure imbalances persist, the rebate is justified. The EU has accepted successive revisions of the UK net contribution, and secured the rebate mechanism with treaty status (i.e. these provisions cannot be cancelled or changed without unanimous agreement, thus including that of the UK).

The fourth issue concerns the funding of the budget, known as its 'own resources'. Over time the structure of funding has changed with an increasing dependence of contributions on a gross national income key. There is a longstanding debate about endowing the EU budget with truly 'own' fiscal resources, beyond the present modest contribution of pooled customs revenues. In this regard the UK government is content with the present balance of competences, in which the idea of granting the EU new taxing powers has little political traction. The most recent attempt to create a new EU tax has been the proposed Financial Transaction ('Tobin') Tax, which the Commission proposed in 2011, but was opposed, notably by the UK and Sweden. As a result 11 member states that supported the proposal decided to proceed with an action under the 'enhanced cooperation' procedure, but this has yet to be definitively agreed.

The fifth issue that receives considerable attention in the review is that of financial management. The British government is concerned that the European Court of Auditors has for many years been refusing to grant complete 'discharge' for the budget, on the grounds that the incidence of 'errors' has been too high. The report notes that the Court of Auditors estimates that there is a 4.8% error rate, which is comparable to the 4.4% error rate found in the US federal budget. The report notes that 'error' and 'fraud' are two different things, and the fraud rate is estimated at a low 0.2% rate. 'Error' is where there has been a degree of non-compliance with EU rules such as for public procurement, or through the incorrect calculation of costs eligible for funding, and such cases are not necessarily fraudulent. The errors are largely committed by the administrations of member states in their execution of about 80% of all EU spending instruments. Yet there remains a problem of public perception, since the Eurobarometer poll shows that three-quarters of EU citizens consider there to be corruption in the EU institutions themselves, for which there is zero evidence.[17]

Assessment

The report notes that stakeholders on the whole considered that "while the balance of competences in the budget was broadly appropriate, the application of these competences could be improved by reform of budget structures, though improving financial management of the EU budget in member states and EU institutions alike and particularly through reform of budget expenditure, focusing on areas of genuine added value" (p.5).

---

[17] The Santer Commission was famously forced to resign by the European Parliament in 1999 for alleged financial mismanagement, but the nearest thing to corruption found was the case of Commissioner Edith Cresson, who hired her dentist as a scientific adviser without following official procedures properly.

British interests have been strongly represented in the evolution of the EU budget, starting, however, from a very disadvantageous initial position upon accession in 1973 when the budget structure adopted before UK accession saw a huge pre-dominance of agricultural spending. This initial disadvantage was largely compensated by the rebate mechanism, while the build-up of the structural funds originated in the regional fund that was strongly advocated by the UK. In recent negotiations the UK has been effective in leading pressure to restrain the growth of the budget for the years ahead until 2020. There have been no new tax competences that the UK would have been doctrinally opposed to, while other ideas such as the Financial Transaction Tax or, more remotely, a specific eurozone budget, would not apply to the UK.

The evidence at a glance – EU budget

EU competence considered broadly appropriate

Major UK complaint over net contribution met by permanent rebate

Long-term structural reform agenda to switch from low to high value added activities (e.g. less agriculture and more research and innovation)

UK achieves reform objectives to reverse growth of real expenditure volume

---

3.5 Taxation

The EU's tax regime is characterised by strong harmonisation of the main indirect taxes (VAT and excises), but much more limited actions in the field of direct taxation. The whole field is covered by the unanimity decision-making rule.

Overall "respondents and interested parties were content with the current balance of competences, taking into account the protections offered by unanimity voting" (p.6). EU level action is judged appropriate where there is an internal market justification and the principles of subsidiarity and proportionality are respected.

The indirect tax regime for VAT has a largely harmonised tax base. Member states retain freedom to set the rates subject to minima (not less 15% for the standard rate, and 5% for reduced rates). Respondents generally welcomed this as ensuring a level playing field in the single market and facilitating cross-border trade. In addition, from accession the UK has enjoyed a special derogation allowing the zero rating for VAT of some products. Excise duties on tobacco, alcohol and energy are subject to minimum rates, but above that the member states are free to set the actual rates. This basic regime for indirect taxes is not contested.

In the fields of direct taxation, both for persons and corporations, the EU's actions have been confined to easing cross-border problems rather than touching the main issues of tax bases and tax rates. There is currently one proposal for a common consolidated corporate tax base (CCCTB) under discussion as a possible action under 'enhanced cooperation'. The UK opposes this, seemingly to avoid any major increase in EU fiscal powers, whereas the case for the CCCTB is to reduce business tax accounting overhead costs and to improve fiscal transparency, without constraining national powers to set tax rates. This proposal has encountered objections from other member states, however, and appears to be stuck.

In the business tax field three measures to lessen obstacles for business across borders are highlighted: the Mergers Directive, the Parent-Subsidiary Directive, and the Interest and Royalties Directive.

The view of respondents was generally to welcome these measures as reducing various tax liabilities hindering cross-border business. Respondents welcomed the role of EU law in enforcing the fundamental freedoms, including the illegality of fiscal discrimination against individuals or corporations on grounds of nationality.

Three particular concerns stand out in the Review. The first concerns the inclusion of tax aspects in various sectoral policy initiatives, which themselves are subject to qualified majority voting. Examples quoted include fiscal aspects of the European Emissions Trading Directive and the Eurovignette Directive for road freight, which were adopted on non-tax legal bases. This is seen as eroding the unanimity principle for taxation.

Second, there is concern over the role of the European Court of Justice. While its positive role in enforcing EU law in the tax area is noted in several decisions, some respondents also view it as making rulings that go beyond its competence, effectively making legislative decisions that escape the veto power of member states, for example in details of the VAT regime. One respondent noted a change in the Court's approach since 2005, however, which attenuates this problem.

Third, there is concern over the use of enhanced cooperation in the tax field, as exemplified by both the CCCTB) idea already mentioned, and the proposed Financial Transaction Tax (FTT). The concern of the City of London is that the FTT would impose requirements on non-participating member states, and the UK in particular because of the size and structure of its financial markets. However, this proposal also seems to be held up amid widespread disagreements over its desirability or feasibility, and the present authors also consider it to be unsound.

There are further detailed concerns regarding the need for timely updating of EU law in the fiscal field and for better impact assessment to accompany proposals.

Assessment

As noted, the overall assessment is that UK respondents find the broad level of EU competences to be about right.

The fundamentals of the EU's tax regime are supported by the respondents; namely limited and clearly demarcated competences in the indirect and direct tax field, and ongoing measures at the level of details to facilitate cross-border business. The UK's strong preference for the unanimity principle in this field is not seriously challenged by the rest of the EU. Neither is the UK's special derogation in the VAT field under any threat. While there has been some debate about creating new 'own resources' for the EU budget, this is not an operationally live issue at present.

The several areas of concern mentioned are typically issues for ongoing negotiation, with a thorough debate of the pros and cons. For example, the present authors would join in criticism of the proposed Financial Transaction Tax, which should be dropped. But we would support the Common Consolidated Corporation Tax Base (CCCTB) proposal, and find the UK's objections unconvincing, especially in view of the new Luxembourg affair (see further, below).

As regards the concern that EU actions under enhanced cooperation risks prejudicing the interests of non-participating EU member states, two comments are in order. On the one hand, procedures are in place to protect the interests of the non-participating member states: there have to be at least nine states to take part in the action, and its authorisation has to be decided unanimously by the Council (Article 329, TFEU)). On the other hand, and even more important for the UK but not made clear in the Review, in the hypothesis of secession these risks would be categorically higher, since from the outside there would be no protection at all.

Postscript. Subsequent to publication of the Review, and shortly after the new Juncker Commission took office on 1 November 2014, the Luxembourg corporation tax affair erupted, under which many multinational corporations (including Amazon, Microsoft, and Apple) had negotiated special tax deals with Luxembourg in exchange for setting up operations there. The lack of coherent tax base policies in Europe has resulted in huge losses of tax revenue for other countries where these companies were operating. But the proposal for the Common Consolidated Corporation Tax Base) is well suited to bring this major anomaly under control, without necessarily affecting tax rates. This would be an important tax reform.

The evidence at a glance – taxation

Respondents content with limited competences, unanimity rule

Harmonised VAT, assures level playing field, not contested

Several useful business tax measures

Financial Transaction Tax proposal opposed by UK and others

Corporation tax base proposal (CCCTB) now, in our view, a plausible reform

---

4. Justice and home affairs

4.1 Fundamental rights*

The 1993 Treaty of Maastricht codified standing case law developed by the EU's Luxembourg-based European Court of Justice (CJEU) in previous decades, stating in Article F that: "The Union shall respect fundamental rights, as guaranteed by the European Convention for the Protection of Human Rights and Fundamental Freedoms signed in Rome on 4 November 1950 and as they result from the constitutional traditions common to the Member States, as general principles of Community law".[18]

The Review on fundamental rights soberly presents a state of play on a topic that has become highly contentious in the political debate. The Review does not concern any specific EU competence on individual rights, since the treaties do not confer express competence on the EU to adopt legislation or to take specific action in this field. Instead, it addresses the EU's overarching competence on fundamental rights. The most important feature of this competence is the obligation resting on the shoulders of the EU, i.e. its institutions *and* the member states in their role as agents of the Union, to respect fundamental rights, which are recognised by the CJEU as general principles of EU law, and reaffirmed in the Charter of Fundamental Rights of the EU.

The Review sets out how the EU legal order protected the fundamental rights of individuals long before the Charter was first proclaimed. The UK government's position is that the Charter did not alter the legal effect (meaning and scope) of fundamental rights in EU law: "they are not two distinct groups of rights in EU law that are potentially subject to disparate interpretations. Both

---

* Section contributed by Steven Blockmans.

[18] To be clear on the 'abc' of the complicated institutional set up, the European Union's Court of Justice CJEU is quite separate from the Strasbourg-based European Court of Human Rights (ECtHR), which is part of the Council of Europe. The Strasbourg Court guards and implements the European Convention for Human Rights (ECHR), which also, however, figures in the jurisprudence of the EU, as the above quote shows, and this text further explains below.

the Charter and the general principles of EU law are part of the EU's primary law. The courts can therefore refer to the Charter and the general principles interchangeably when applying fundamental rights to EU institutions and member states" (p. 34). This view is largely reflected in the evidence.

The most contentious issue discussed in the Review concerns the question of whether Protocol 30 to the Lisbon Treaty (on the Application of the Charter of Fundamental Rights of the European Union to Poland and the United Kingdom) presents an opt-out of the Charter. The Review states that "the Protocol is not, and never has been, an opt-out for the UK from the application of the Charter" (p.25). While it only applies to the UK and Poland (the Czech Republic having rescinded its initial inclusion under the Protocol) its purpose is rather to clarify, in legally binding terms, how the Charter applies to the EU institutions and member states. The UK government's position is that the Charter reaffirms the rights, freedoms and principles recognised in EU law, but does not create new rights or principles. This view is almost unanimously supported in the evidence and is consistent with the preamble to the Charter itself.

Chapter 4 of the Review is of most interest as it summarises the wide range of evidence submitted on the impact on the UK of the EU's competence on fundamental rights, in the following terms. "Beyond recognition that when [EU institutions and member states (within the scope of EU law)] act they should do so consistently with some form of human rights protection, [the evidence shows] little consensus on what constitutes the UK interest in this context. Views on whether the EU's competence on fundamental rights is being exercised consistently with the interests of the UK vary depending on perspectives on the role of supranational human rights mechanisms and national sovereignty" (p.45).

This is particularly evident in the widely differing assessments of how the ECJ exercises its jurisdiction in high-profile cases, with the following formulations quoted in the report: from "naked grab of territory by the [CJEU]" to "there is little or no evidence of competence creep", and "the protection afforded to citizens' fundamental rights by the CJEU is insufficient when balanced against the rights enjoyed by business under EU law" (p.48).

Whereas EU law contains a wider array of rights than those protected under the UK's 1998 Human Rights Act or the 1950 Convention (ECHR), the evidence presented in the report indicates that EU fundamental rights have so far had a limited impact on domestic case law. Yet, respondents from civil society, academia and the legal profession have suggested that the EU guarantees that could offer a greater standard of protection are the right to a fair hearing (especially in the sphere of immigration and asylum) and the prohibition on discrimination.

An inherent problem with the multi-layered order of fundamental rights protection is that this partially overlapping system compromises legal certainty. Moreover, the complexity of the system means that enforcing fundamental rights is expensive for both litigants and the public purse. The evidence collected in the report nevertheless indicates a high degree of consistency between the level of protection afforded by EU fundamental rights and that afforded by the Convention. In part this is due to the CJEU following the jurisprudence of the Strasbourg Court.

As a founding member of the Council of Europe, the UK was one of the first to sign the Convention and it has been an ardent supporter of the Strasbourg-based court for decades. However, in recent years, a number of deeply unpopular judgments have sparked complaints against the overall binding nature of ECtHR judgments on British law, notably declaring illegal the ban on prisoners in jail from voting in elections, and the barring the deportation of alleged al-Qaeda terrorist Abu Qatada (who was repeatedly imprisoned but never prosecuted for any crime). With the rise of UKIP and anti-immigration sentiment, a storm has been brewing over 'European' oversight of the UK's human rights track record.

Subsequent to the publication of the Review, an eight-page strategy paper of the Conservative Party (i.e. not the government) was published in October 2014 entitled "Protecting Human Rights in the UK", in relation to which Justice Secretary Chris Grayling of the Conservatives stated: "We can no longer tolerate this mission creep. What we have effectively got is a legal blank cheque, where the court can go where it chooses to go. We will put in place a provision that will say that the rulings of Strasbourg will not have legal effect in the UK without the consent of parliament.

Effectively, what we are doing is turning Strasbourg into an advisory body."[19]

Grayling added that a new Conservative government (i.e. without the coalition with the Liberal Democrats) would withdraw from the ECHR if Parliament failed to secure the right to veto judgments from the ECtHR. Prime Minister Cameron had summarised the policy at a party conference in Birmingham in September 2014: "Let me put this very clearly: we do not require instruction on this from judges in Strasbourg."

Arguments about the alleged undue influence of the Court on national matters may be put into perspective with some statistics from the Strasbourg court. Between 1959 and 2013, the number of judgments involving the UK totalled 499 judgments, of which only 3% were found against the British government. By comparison, France has had 913 cases, Russia 1,475 (since 1996), Italy 2,268, and Turkey 2,994. The number of cases found against the UK is both quite small and arguably of secondary gravity compared to the many arising in Russia or Turkey. However, the collateral damage done to the ECtHR by the UK's withdrawal could be of major importance, with Russia and others exploiting the precedent.

Assessment

The evidence gathered by this Review shows that there is broad consensus that respect for human rights is in the national interest of the UK, which in 2015 proudly celebrates the 800th anniversary of the Magna Carta. As much as the EU fundamental rights system has been deemed beneficial to all sectors in the UK because it keeps the EU in check, so too is the ECtHR's primary function to provide external (independent, impartial and expert) scrutiny to prevent any member state from acting or mandating to act in a manner that is inconsistent with 21st century levels of human rights protection in Europe.

Conservative Party threats to withdraw from the Convention and ECHR are, in our view, a populist overreaction to

---

[19] www.theguardian.com/politics/interactive/2014/oct/03/conservatives-human-rights-act-full-document

a handful of adverse rulings from the Strasbourg Court and would be a major reversal of the human rights cause in Europe as a whole. The idea that the status of the Court's judgments could be reduced to advice for the British parliament has no chance of general acceptance by the member states in the Council of Europe.

Withdrawal from the Convention would link into the debate about Britain's possible exit from the EU. After all, respect for the rights and freedoms as guaranteed by the ECHR, as part of the general principles of EU law, is one of the pre-conditions for EU membership. Domestic protection of rights and freedoms under a new British Bill of Rights and Responsibilities might be less than under the Convention, and thus raise the question whether it was good enough to continue to satisfy EU membership criteria.

In other words, while the Conservative Party's target is mainly the ECtHR in Strasbourg, secession from the Convention there could have highly complicated and damaging impacts on the UK's relations with the EU, as well as undermining the general human rights system in Europe as a whole.

Postscript. The Lisbon Treaty sought to clarify the relationship between the EU and the Strasbourg Court by deciding in Article 6 TEU that: "The Union shall accede to the European Convention for the Protection of Human Rights and Fundamental Freedoms. Such accession shall not affect the Union's competences as defined in the Treaties". Negotiations between the EU and the Council of Europe were therefore undertaken, and a draft agreement was drawn up. Subsequent to publication of this Review, however, in December 2014 the CJEU declared this draft agreement to be incompatible with EU law on a number of grounds (Opinion 2/13). This leads into complex legal arguments that have been analysed elsewhere.[20] Suffice here to observe that the draft agreement is now at least put on hold, possibly indefinitely.

---

[20] Adam Lazowski and Ramses A. Wessel, "The European Court of Justice blocks the EU's accession to the ECHR3", CEPS Commentary, 8 January 2015.

> *The evidence at a glance – fundamental rights*
> UK a strong supporter of human rights, going back to the Magna Carta
> EU law links to Council of Europe's Convention and Court
> A few Strasbourg judgments against UK prompts Tory ire
> Secession from Strasbourg would spill over into EU competence
> It would also damage the human rights system in wider Europe

4.2   Civil judicial cooperation*

The broad area of Freedom, Security and Justice is relatively new and fast-growing area of EU competence, driven by the combination of suppression of border controls within the Schengen area, alongside the manifest growth of cross-border crime and international terrorism. Cooperation started in the justice and home affairs domain in 1975 with the inter-governmental Trevi Group that saw however no EU competence. The 1992 Maastricht Treaty brought it into EU competence under the Third Pillar, where however the process remained essentially inter-governmental with no role for the Commission or European Parliament. But then the 1997 Amsterdam Treaty and 2009 Lisbon Treaty progressively moved the whole domain into the mainstream EU shared competences. With the Lisbon Treaty the Third Pillar was finally abolished and all police and criminal law matters are now subject to regular QMV voting in the Council and jurisdiction of the CJEU. The UK negotiated special opt-out provisions in both the Amsterdam and Lisbon Treaties, and in Protocol 21 of the Lisbon Treaty the UK has a general opt-out, coupled to the possibility to opt-in selectively on a case-by-case basis.

Civil judicial cooperation is one of the chapters of Title V of the Lisbon Treaty (TFEU) that defines the EU's competences in the Area of Freedom, Security and Justice.[21] According to Protocol 21

---

* Section contributed by Steve Peers.

[21] Other chapters concern border checks, asylum and immigration, and police cooperation. See the next two sections, below.

the whole of this area however sees the UK, with Ireland, having opted out of the EU's actions, unless they specifically request to opt in on an itemised basis. This is the essential background to the discussion that follows on where the UK's participation can be considered advantageous or not.

The contributors to this Review took different views as to whether the EU's measures in this area were an improvement on intergovernmental cooperation. One group of contributors argued that they were, on the grounds that the UK would have difficulty replicating the results by means of bilateral arrangements with member states. A smaller group argued the contrary.

Many contributors agreed with the scope of Article 81 TFEU (the legal base for measures in this field), although others were worried that it left too much scope for measures that were not limited to cross-border cooperation.

Most contributors were supportive of the flagship measure in this area, the Brussels I Regulation, which has the effect of promoting English law for international contracts, and ensures legal certainty and enforceability of judgments in international disputes. There was some concern about certain judgments of the Court of Justice of the European Union (CJEU) on the regulation, for example with respect to arbitration disputes, third-country jurisdiction and choice-of-court clauses in contracts, but those concerns had been addressed by recent amendments to the legislation.

Many also supported the EU regulations on the choice of law in contract and in tort, although some had doubts about their uniform interpretation, or the problems that would arise if a foreign court tried to interpret English law.

As for EU family law rules, most stated that the Brussels II Regulation had simplified cross-border divorce proceedings, but it was still open to litigants to 'rush to court' rather than consider mediation. The rules in the regulation regarding children were also broadly supported, although they could be improved for children in care or with foster families. Some had doubts about EU rules on maintenance proceedings, since their interaction with the rules on divorce could be complex.

There were also views about other measures: support for the evidence regulation; opposing views about the usefulness of the legislation on service of documents; and support for the potential use of the small claims regulation and the mediation directive. There was a general view that awareness of these measures should be raised, since the available statistics showed that they were not used very often. There was also support for the regulation on insolvency proceedings.

Some contributors were critical of certain judgments of the CJEU on civil law matters, suggesting improvements in the Court's proceedings.

A large majority of contributors took the view that the EU measures in this area were helpful for the single market, given that they promoted legal certainty in the context of cross-border trade relationships and contracts.

Most contributors supported the opt-out for the UK, although some disagreed with its use in particular cases. For instance, some legal associations wanted the UK to opt in to the latest justice programme, and the succession regulation.

Opinions were divided about the EU's external role in this area, given that it often has exclusive external competence to enter into agreements in this field. A number of contributors questioned the Commission's claim that the EU has exclusive competence to decide on the extension of The Hague Convention on child abduction to new countries (as far as member states are concerned), or complained about the delay in EU ratification of international treaties.

Finally, as for future measures, contributors called for the EU to focus on reform and consolidation of existing rules, rather than the development of new measures affecting civil law and family law more generally.

Assessment

The overwhelming majority of contributors appeared to support civil law cooperation as an important issue linked to the single market for business and trade and (as regards family law) the movement of persons. This support no doubt wane if it were not for the UK's opt-out, which has enabled it either to stay entirely outside of measures that it considered undesirable, or at least to 'hedge its bets' by staying out when a measure was first proposed, and then opting in after its adoption if it was satisfied with the result. There were some doubts, however, as to whether this approach was sustainable in the long term.

Having said that, British contributors have a number of detailed suggestions to improve the EU measures that would facilitate the accomplishment of their objectives, particularly in cases involving divorce and children. Awareness-raising would increase the public use of these measures.

It should be noted that some of the issues raised by contributors have been addressed in practice. As the contributors themselves noted, the recent amendments to the Brussels I Regulation addressed many of the complaints that practitioners had about the CJEU's case law. It would seem that when British practitioners make a detailed and reasonable critique of an EU measure, they can be successful in convincing others in the EU to share their point of view.

A number of issues raised in this part of the Balance of Competences Review have also been addressed since it was carried out. The issue of competence regarding extension of The Hague Convention on child abduction should soon be resolved by the CJEU, after that Court held a hearing on the issue earlier this year. In late 2013, the Commission proposed amendments to the small claims regulation to improve its use, including a large increase in the threshold for application of that regulation. The EU has now ratified The Hague Convention on maintenance, and the Commission has recently proposed that it ratify The Hague Convention on choice-of-court clauses, which will bring that Convention into force. A proposal to improve the insolvency regulation is also under discussion. The Commission recently began a public consultation on improving the rules on child abduction and divorce jurisdiction, the CJEU has now been seized with cases concerning the maintenance regulation, which might clarify the issues concerning interpretation of that regulation, and there is no sign that the EU legislature will take a broad view of the scope of competence under Article 81 and apply it to proceedings that do not have a cross-border element.

All in all, the UK has been able to select from the civil proceedings measures those which are best adapted to the common law system (and the Scottish hybrid system) and which best serve the needs of British business and the legal profession. It has also been able to shape the amendment of those measures when necessary, and avoid their application if it disagreed with them.

The evidence at a glance – civil judicial cooperation

UK secured a block opt-out, with possibility for selective opt-ins

UK enjoys exceptional flexibility in EU to pick and choose

Majority support for civil law cooperation on single market matters

Detailed proposals for improvements of EU measures

4.3 Police and criminal law cooperation[*]

The contributors to the Review in this area address the overlapping issues of the UK's opt-out and the usefulness of individual measures. Some support changing the longstanding government position (dating from the original JHA opt-out in 1999) that the UK should decide to use the opt-out on a case-by-case basis, either by switching to opting in as the default measure, or to opting out as the default measure (a detailed account of this debate is found on pages 33-38 of the Review). In our opinion such a change would be possible without treaty amendment, and could take the form either of a political commitment by the government, or of specific provisions in an Act of Parliament. It would also be possible to adopt the Irish system, where each decision to opt in has to be approved by Parliament.

The case for a default opt-in is that it would increase goodwill towards the UK among other member states, while leaving flexibility for the government to opt out in individual cases where the criteria for doing so are met. It would also make the government's decisions more consistent and transparent.

---

[*] Section contributed by Steve Peers.

The group supporting a default opt-out points to cases where the UK was able to ensure that it was satisfied with measures before opting in, and observes that the UK was still able to influence the content of discussions because other member states were anxious to have the UK participate, by means of opting in to a measure after its adoption. However, there have been a relatively modest number of such cases, i.e. where the UK opted out but indicated that it might still opt in after adoption. In one such case (a civil law regulation on succession), the UK negotiated its position at length but ultimately decided not to opt in; this might well have lost it some goodwill among other member states. Moving to a default opt-out strategy might also lose the UK some of its influence in this area and, in particular, a more frequent use of the strategy of opting out of measures to which the UK would actually prefer to opt in could irritate other member states greatly.

As for specific measures in this area, contributors reserved particular criticism for the proposed Regulations on Europol (due to the rules on access to police information); the European Public Prosecutor's Office (EPPO); and Eurojust (due to the links between Eurojust and the EPPO). In practice, however, the UK's concerns on the first of these measures seem to have been addressed during the negotiations.

There were mixed views on EU legislation regarding issues such as criminal procedure, substantive criminal law and mutual recognition. On criminal procedure, some supported it in principle, some were opposed in principle and some believed that insufficient account had been taken of practical questions, particularly the directive on interpretation and translation for criminal suspects. This points to a greater need for the legal profession and other practitioners to put across their points of view during negotiations.

On substantive criminal law, there was concern in the Review about the tendency in a few recent measures to include proposals for minimum sentences. However, it should be noted that the provisions in question were removed during negotiations in the Council. Others pointed to United Nations treaties in this area. It should be noted, however, that the EU is party to some of the treaties referred to (notably the UN Convention on organised crime and its protocols) and much EU law aims to implement the other treaties (such as the Lanzarote Convention on offences against children) in detail. The latter Convention is in any event still not in force in nine member states: Cyprus, the Czech Republic, Estonia, Germany, Hungary, Ireland, Poland, Slovakia and the United Kingdom. Also, there are no international treaties on some of the issues addressed by EU law, such as environmental crime and fraud against the EU budget.

On mutual recognition, some pointed instead to the international legal framework (Council of Europe) or to bilateral arrangements, as an alternative. On the first point, it should be noted that some issues are not governed by the Council of Europe system, such as pre-trial supervision. Other issues are regulated by Council of Europe treaties, which a limited number of member states have ratified, i.e. probation and parole and mutual recognition of criminal convictions. A third category of issues is indeed regulated by Council of Europe treaties, which all member states have ratified (extradition, mutual assistance, transfer of prisoners), but those treaties are a patchwork, since there are protocols that not all states have ratified, and there are a large number of reservations and options within each Convention. By comparison, EU measures have fewer options and deadlines to take action, resulting in (for instance) a huge increase in the number of people extradited between member states, and a much shorter time period for the average extradition.

On the second point, it is doubtful whether a series of bilateral agreements with member states is a realistic alternative. The existence of EU measures in this area gives rise to EU external competence in the field, which might possibly be exclusive to some extent (there is no CJEU case law on this issue yet). The same rules apply to bilateral agreements between member states (see the CJEU's *Pringle* judgment). So it would be necessary to negotiate a treaty between the UK and the EU as a whole (assuming that the EU can sign a treaty at all with a member state), or for the EU to authorise its member states to sign treaties with the UK as regards the issues concerned.

Regarding the role of the CJEU, opinions were again mixed, with some supporting the role of the Court in this field and some raising fears that the Court would interfere too much in national legal systems. In effect, the Court has been delivering judgments on criminal law issues since 2001, since about two-thirds of member states opted in to the Court's jurisdiction under the arrangements set out in the Treaty of Amsterdam. Critics of the Court's jurisdiction do not point to any particular judgment to justify their argument. Any change to the Court's jurisdiction would require a treaty amendment.

Finally, the summary of the law in this area is not fully accurate. In the event that the UK seeks to opt in to a measure after it has been adopted, there is no treaty provision that gives the Commission the power to "impos[e] conditions" (point 1.30). Equally, in the event of a Commission refusal to let the UK opt in, a possible UK appeal to the Council is not limited to objecting to such conditions. Rather, Article 331 TFEU states that the Commission shall "note where necessary that any conditions of participation have been fulfilled"; this can only be a reference to the "conditions of participation" laid down in the original Council Decision authorising enhanced cooperation, as occurs Article 328 TFEU.

Postcript. Following the murderous attack in Paris on the staff of *Charlie Hebdo* magazine on 7 January 2015, an intensification of EU measures on police and criminal law matters seems likely. The UK will remain able to decide on whether to opt in to each measure on a case by case basis. It might also be useful to review whether the UK should opt in to some existing EU measures that concern the fight against terrorism. However, at first sight the UK already seems to apply all relevant EU measures, except for the substantive criminal laws concerning terrorism offences, which in any event match UK domestic law.

Assessment

All in all, the UK has been able to select from EU criminal law those measures that are best adapted to the common law system (and the Scottish hybrid system) and which it believes are advantageous to cooperation with other member states. There has been no case of the UK being outvoted (in practice, despite the extension of qualified majority voting, criminal law measures are not pushed through against a member state's opposition), and no judgment of the CJEU that contradicts the principles of the UK criminal justice system has been identified.

The evidence at a glance: police and criminal law cooperation

A growing domain of EU policy, driven by manifest threats of terrorism and cross-border crime.

Opt-out and opt-in arrangements for the UK allows for a best fit with its common law system.

Variants among opt-out/opt-in systems discussed, with these options remaining open to UK.

No cases of UK being outvoted, or contradicting its criminal justice system.

Alternatives such as relying on the Council of Europe or bilateral treaties appear less adequate.

4.4 Asylum and non-EU immigration

This Review deals with border controls, asylum and immigration, which involve shared competences of the EU and member states, and is an important part of the EU's broader Area of Freedom, Security and Justice. This is an area with substantial growth of the content of EU competences over the last decades.

The present legal basis is set out in Articles 77 to 79 of the TFEU, which empowers the EU to minimise border controls, adopt a common visa policy and measures on passports, and develop a common asylum policy and a common immigration policy.

The strategic basis for this complex of policies originated in the decision taken in 1985 by continental EU states to abolish frontier controls in the Schengen system, whereas the UK and Ireland opted to retain their national border controls, given their island geography. While the Schengen system originally lay outside the EU treaties, it is now fully integrated in EU law (Article 77 of TFEU), and the UK's opt-out is enshrined in Protocol No. 20 of the TFEU.

With regard to asylum and immigration policies (Articles 78 and 79 of TFEU) the UK, along with Ireland, enjoys special provisions (under Protocol 21 of TFEU) under which it is only bound by EU legal acts if it chooses to opt in. Even if the UK chooses not to opt in when a measure is introduced it retains the option to do so at any later stage, subject to Commission approval.

Border controls. The UK does not participate in core features of the Schengen system, namely the Schengen Borders Code establishing common external border checks, or the Visa Information System (VIS), which is a database to serve security purposes. It partly participates in the Schengen Information System (SIS), which is used to issue alerts over suspected criminals. These limitations mean that UK security interests may not be optimised. The UK does participate in some other Schengen measures, such as the Advance Passenger Information Directive, and the Carriers Liability law. The UK also has limited involvement in the workings of the FRONTEX agency, and may do so also with the European Border Surveillance System (Eurosur). The UK has opted in to the Biometrics Residence Permit Regulation.

Asylum. European norms for the handling of asylum seekers originated with the Dublin Convention of 1990, which, however, was an intergovernmental agreement of the then 12 member states outside EU law, whose core principle was that an asylum seeker has to be handled by the member state he/she first enters. Following the rapid growth of EU competences in this area a revised version of the Dublin Convention was integrated into EU law in 2003 ('Dublin II'). A related development was the creation of the EURODAC, namely a biometric fingerprint database to enable individual member states to verify whether asylum seekers have already applied elsewhere. The UK has opted in to both Dublin II and EURODAC. The UK is currently making use of an important European Court of Human Rights ruling that refines the basic Dublin rule, in saying that asylum seekers should only be returned to the country of first entry if there are no "systemic deficiencies" in that state's capacity to handle the asylum seekers properly; as a result, the UK does not currently return asylum seekers to Greece. On the other hand, the UK has not opted in to other measures such as the Reception Conditions Directive, the Qualifications Directive or the Asylum Procedures Directive.

Immigration. The EU has legislation creating certain funds for dealing with immigration, but the UK has not opted in to the External Borders Fund, for example. The EU makes readmission agreements with many countries, and the UK opts in to many of these, but not all. The UK has not opted in to a set of nine directives concerning criteria for acceptance of migrants, including the Blue Card system for highly qualified persons and other detailed provisions concerning social security rights of immigrants and measures to counter illegal migration. The UK government generally feels that details of its own rules are better suited to its needs and perceptions.

Overall, this is a complex set of policies where the UK has negotiated a status quo characterised by large-scale opt-outs, together with various continuing opt-in possibilities; i.e. a remarkable combination of selectivity and flexibility. The Review reports that the UK has chosen to opt in to roughly one-third of EU measures in this whole field, with fewer more recently, however, as the EU has extended its activities. The opt-in/out arrangements allow for successive adjustments of the UK's relationship with the core EU that in principle mean that it can choose, to a high degree unilaterally, its optimal policy package, and to recalibrate it at times. This selectivity and flexibility has to be considered a privilege, since the EU knows full well that a generalisation of these options would make the system unworkable to the point of disintegration. For this reason the EU is in principle extremely reluctant to agree to measures that are commonly described as 'cherry-picking'. The island geography of the UK and Ireland provides some objective foundations for this special deal, however.

Assessment

Given the UK's strategic non-participation in the Schengen system and related matters of border controls and immigration policy, subject only to some specific elements of cooperation with the EU, this Review chose not to assess whether the EU's overall competences in these fields was appropriate. The Review notes that for the UK the balance of competences in these areas lies mainly with the UK itself, and the government does not intend to change this. The Review concentrates on assessing whether the UK's opt-outs and special provisions are in the national interest.

The Review reiterates the UK government's view that, while these large exclusions from EU competences entail certain costs, they are largely outweighed by the benefits of enhanced border security. While this cost-benefit conclusion appears to be of an assertion than based on evidence, there is little argument to the contrary presented by independent stakeholders. Moreover, the Review notes that the opt-outs are largely supported by public opinion.

On various details, even from a purely British standpoint, there may be grounds for debating whether the UK has optimised all its options in this area. For example, while the keeping of border controls is generally supported in the UK, the costs to the tourist sector and the transport industry of having a separate visa system are seen as being considerable: a visa mutual recognition agreement between the EU and the Schengen system might cut these costs without the UK losing control of its borders (the UK might accept foreign travellers with Schengen visas, for example).

Although not discussed in this Review, it is evident that the Schengen system is also largely supported by public opinion on the European continent. For the founding EU member states it would now be considered unthinkable that a motorist from the Netherlands to Italy should again have to pass frontier controls at the Belgian, Luxembourg, and French or German frontiers, for example. For the new member states the freedom of frontier controls is highly valued, for both practical reasons and as embodiment of the European ideal. There is thus no basic questioning of the EU's competences in this broad field, and on the contrary a determination by the Schengen states to deepen their common policies in the Freedom, Security and Justice Area. But this does not depend on the UK.

The evidence at a glance – asylum and non-EU immigration
UK stakeholders content with opt-out from Schengen zone
Further opt-outs also for asylum and immigration rules
But selective opt-back-ins (some asylum rules and biometric data)
UK secured a remarkable combination of selectivity and flexibility

5.   Education, research and culture

5.1   Education, vocational training and youth

The EU has a 'supporting competence' in the broad field of education, which means that national policies predominate. This attribution of competences is not contested in the UK or elsewhere in the EU. The EU's activities in this domain fall into three very different categories, i) policy coordination under the so-called Open Method of Coordination (OMC), which is based on 'soft law' or non-binding guidelines and peer review, ii) the directly operational mobility programmes funded by the EU budget, notably Erasmus+, and iii) voluntary mutual recognition frameworks for vocational qualifications. The evolution of these various types of competence has proceeded in a pragmatic manner with relatively little EU legislation and correspondingly little political controversy. Overall, the UK and other member states remain free to make their own laws and policies in the area of education, and are also free to enter into bilateral or multilateral international agreements as long as these do not override specific EU competences.

Policy coordination in the areas of education and training has acquired a higher profile since 2000 under the influence of the 'Lisbon strategy', which set objectives for the period 2000 to 2010 as a competitive knowledge-based economy, to raise the employment rate, and thus contribute to overall economic growth. This was followed by 'Europe 2020', proposed in 2010 for the following ten-year period, with advances in education forming a central part of the strategy. This initiative could not be based on legislative action by the EU in the field of education, however, since that would have meant radically increasing EU competences in this field, which for member states was out of the question. The choice was therefore to rely on the OMC. Under this method the Europe 2020 strategy set many targets in the educational area, such as for 95% of children to participate in early childhood education before compulsory schooling; 40% of people to complete some form of higher education; 15% of adults to participate in life-long learning, etc. Member states are expected to set national targets consistent with these EU-level targets.

All member states except the UK did so, many of them placing the targets at the heart of their educational reform programmes. For its part the UK declined on grounds that the target-setting was not in line with UK government policy and that it was not appropriate for the EU to set targets in areas in which it did not have competence. The comment of one respondent was "the UK has chosen to be more on the margins rather than [at] the centre" of the European education agenda (p.32). There is certainly a wider debate on how far the EU's target-setting is an effective instrument of policy in this field, but here the UK has secured another opt-out to suit its political preference, albeit a less prominent one because the instruments of EU action in question are 'soft' rather than hard law.

On the other hand, the UK has been at the heart of the Bologna process, initiated in 1998 by the education ministers of France, Germany, Italy and the UK. This is a voluntary inter-governmental process outside the EU framework, and is extended to include 47 European countries. Its flagship achievement has been to establish norms for the three basic levels of higher education qualifications: Bachelors, Masters and Doctorates, and so facilitate comparability and exchange between university systems.

The EU's flagship project in the education field is undoubtedly its student mobility programmes, notably Erasmus, which has been highly operational and even of transformative importance. The expression 'Erasmus generation' has been coined to refer to the young Europeans who are part of the new 'normal', in which a university student spends a year of studies away from his or her home country. Erasmus was started in the 1980s and built up through several iterations, with various programmes consolidated in 2014 under the 'Erasmus+' banner. The budget of €14.7 billion for Erasmus+ for the seven-year 2014-2020 period represents an increase of 40% over the previous budgetary period, which the British government views as a successful example of shifting the budget more into activities where the EU contributes high added value. The majority of the Review respondents "were strongly in favour of managing and funding mobility programmes at the EU level" (p.40).

Recent statistics show that 14,607 UK students and 2,178 academic staff spent the year 2012-2013 at universities in other EU countries. Numbers have been rising steadily. At the same time there are almost twice as many students from other EU countries visiting the UK (25,750 in 2011-2012). The reasons for this imbalance seem plausibly related to the English language factor, with its value as a second language for students from other EU countries, while the poor foreign language competence of UK students limits their opportunities to study abroad (a survey of 14 EU countries reported in the Review shows UK students to be 'bottom of the class' in foreign language skills, p.38).

As regards the practical impact of the Erasmus programme on individual participants, results of a survey are cited in which 64% of employers consider international experience to be important when recruiting employees, while participants in the Erasmus programme are half as likely to suffer long-term unemployment compared to non-participants, and more likely to start their own businesses (p.41).

The EU is active in the area of vocational education and training, but here the accent is on voluntary frameworks conducive to the mutual recognition of professional qualifications. These include the European Qualifications Framework (EQF), the European Credit Transfer and Accumulation System (ECTS), the Europass and others.

The Review notes the administrative burdens of EU programmes, summed up as follows: "While there was recognition of the need for appropriate controls to ensure both value for money and propriety, there was also the near universal belief that these goals could be achieved with reduced and more streamlined administrative burdens" (p.56).

Assessment

While the education sector covers a wide spectrum of EU activity, ranging from highly operational 'niche' activities, notably for student mobility, through to policy engagement aiming at such strategic objectives as a competitive knowledge-based economy, there are no real disagreements over the EU's competences in this field. The 'niche' activities for student mobility are valued highly, with the UK profiting considerably because of its strong university system and English language advantage. On the other hand, activity aimed at fundamental educational policy objectives is kept securely in the field of national policy competence, and subject mainly to peer review and comparative analysis. To the extent that the UK is wary that such activity might see the EU creeping into national competence, it has itself opted out of the setting of targets under the Europe 2020 programme, whereas all other member states are moving ahead with this. Broad issues of higher education models and reform are also pursued under the Bologna Process, which is a voluntary inter-governmental activity outside and wider than the EU, with which the UK is comfortable. EU activity in the field of vocational training is also essentially voluntary.

For these reasons, while the education field represents a differentiated set of elements, overall the current national-EU balance of competences is one that suits the UK quite well.

The evidence at a glance – education & vocational training

Education a 'supporting competence' of the EU; the primary competence of member states is not challenged

EU activities span a broad range under this 'supporting' competence:

- Overall educational policy issues subject to 'soft law', i.e. non-binding guidelines and peer review

- Erasmus+ as a major operational mobility programme, and valued 'niche' activity

- Vocational training objectives pursued through voluntary frameworks

---

5.2   Research and space

The UK prides itself on having a highly competitive research capacity in a wide range of fields. The UK does exceptionally well at winning EU research funding, and under the current seven-year budget (2007-2013, Framework Programme 7, or FP7) it has received €6.1 billion, or 15.4% of the total, second only to Germany's share of 16.1%.

The EU's legal basis for action in the research area is its 'shared competence'. However, it is an unusual hybrid variant on the standard shared competence in that it does not limit the competence of member states to act in this field. Prior to the Lisbon Treaty the EU's competence was in a supporting capacity only. While the Lisbon Treaty was in theory upgrading this into a shared competence, the hybrid factor has limited the significance of this change. The Review comments that this has added rather than removed confusion around the competence question.

In concrete terms, however, the EU is increasingly influencing strategic decisions about which research area to prioritise through the weight of its funding programmes. The FP7 programme has had a budget of €50.5 billion, making it the world's largest research programme. The ten priority sectors covered are quite vast in extent: health, food, agriculture and fisheries, biotechnology, information and communications technologies, nanosciences, nanotechnologies, materials and new production technologies, energy, environment including climate change, transport including aeronautics, socio-economic sciences and the humanities, space, and security.

The EU's latest research programme for the years 2014-2020, (Framework Programme 8, dubbed 'Horizon 2020') has a larger budget than ever, with €79 billion. Its priorities are placed under the headings of excellent science, enabling technologies to support industry, and a number of European and global challenges such as energy security, food security and climate change.

The Lisbon Treaty also embraced the idea of the European Research Area (ERA), which is an umbrella concept for promoting mobility among European scientists and researchers, and reinforced partnerships between member states and the Commission's programmes. The added value of this concept, beyond the major operating programmes, is not so clear, however.

The EU has a longstanding competence in the field of space, funding flagship projects such as the Galileo satellite programme, and the Copernicus programme that undertakes environmental monitoring from space. The European Space Agency (ESA) is a major partner for the EU, but it is institutionally separate from the EU. Integration of the ESA into EU structures has been discussed, but is not currently being pursued. In the latest call for space projects under the FP7 around 80% of successful bids include a UK partner and around 24% are led by a UK partner.

There is a significant international cooperation dimension to the Framework Programmes, with 13 countries having made agreements with the EU to participate in projects and contribute to the budget.

The Review reported widespread stakeholder frustration with the heavy bureaucratic procedures involved in applying for grants, in the programming of deliverables, and reporting requirements. The Review further suggested that stakeholders may have to advocate recourse to the simpler arrangements that might come with national funding, but that this case was not made. There was recognition that a certain degree of bureaucracy was unavoidable to ensure fair completion and minimise fraud; national funding has its own bureaucracy, of course, and there was no certainty that under a national funding regime comparable resources would be made available. Most stakeholders seemed confident that the Commission was addressing these problems and that improvements were anticipated under Horizon 2020.

A strong message from stakeholders is that the UK's reputation with international partners, both in business and research, is enhanced by being part of the EU. Views were expressed to the effect that 'the European brand can also give an additional guarantee in dealings with parties in non-EU countries', and that EU funding made it possible to build more international partnerships than otherwise would have been possible.

Assessment

The Review's summary assessment was as follows: "The majority of respondents felt that a combination of local, national, EU, bilateral and international policies and collaborations was the most effective way of managing the complex needs of differing research fields. To this end, current arrangements, while not perfect, were broadly considered or provide a good foundation" (p.6).

The present authors' experience of European research institutes working in the social sciences highlights two points. First, it is true that the bureaucratic burden of EU funding procedures is disagreeable for the grantee; by comparison funding from private foundations is a rather different experience because such foundations generally set out much simpler project funding criteria. It is important that the Commission try to simplify procedures without prejudicing the academic objectivity and freedom from national bias in decisions. At the same time, we acknowledge that the Framework Programmes are generally thought to be well protected against unfair bias through the use of independent assessors, and the rigorous financial reporting requirements are an effective barrier to corruption.

Secondly, the Review perhaps fails to underline sufficiently how in the space of a few decades the European research area has effectively come into being, replacing the prior system of national research communities that were largely operating in isolation from each other. The community of European researchers is nowadays highly integrated. This is now taken for granted; any idea of reverting to the old regime of nationally segmented research structures receives little or no support.

The evidence at a glance – research and space

Balance of competences (national, EU and international) broadly sound

UK strong beneficiary from EU research funding

Frustrations over heavy bureaucratic procedures

UK reputation with international partners enhanced by EU

5.3   Culture, tourism and sport

The EU's competences in the fields of culture, tourism and sport are relatively new. The Lisbon Treaty provides that they are all "supporting competences" (TFEU, Articles 165, 167 and 195), which means that while the EU may decide certain actions under these headings, this does not restrict what the member states decide under their own competences.

Culture. It is explicitly excluded that the EU legislate in order to harmonise national laws in the field of culture. The EU's main actions in this field include the MEDIA programme for supporting the European film industry, and the European programme to digitise cultural materials in European libraries and museums. The British Museum, for example, contributes to the Europeana programme, which now includes 1.5 million digital assets from the UK. Other measures include the Cultural Objects Directive (93/7/EEC), which provides a cooperative procedure for returning national treasures that have been unlawfully removed from a member state. The Capitals for Culture programme, from which Glasgow and Liverpool have been beneficiaries, has been particularly appreciated.

The report says that "The 30 contributors from the culture sector were the most unequivocal in their support of EU activity under its competence" (p.27), with various contributors stressing the comparative success of UK cultural organisations in securing EU funding. There was emphasis on how the bringing together of cultural communities across member states delivers benefits that are not achievable at national level, and on how such programmes could achieve a critical mass allowing the UK and European partners to compete on the global stage and project 'soft power'.

Tourism. Actions in this sector are not very extensive. There are several measures effectively protecting the rights of travellers and tourists, such as the Denied Boarding Regulation protecting air travellers in the event of delays, and the Package Travel Directive, which protects consumers in the event of a travel operator going into liquidation.

The European Tour Operators Association noted the risk that the UK's self-exclusion from the Schengen visa system may have a negative impact on the UK tourist sector, through the UK being dropped out of multi-country itineraries.

Overall, contributors felt that the impact of EU measures in this field were quite modest.

Sport. In this there have been some important specific measures, influenced by the case law of the European Court of Justice relating to the free movement of workers. In particular, as a result of the Bosman case in 2005, UEFA and FIFA were obliged to make far-reaching changes to their regulations on transfer systems for footballers, preventing restrictions on the freedom of footballers to move clubs once their contracts expire. In the broadcasting domain the Audiovisual Media Services Directive (2010/13/EU) lists major events that are to be made available for free TV viewing, including major football, rugby, athletic and golfing championships. The huge increase in following of European football championships makes it essential that there be organised discussions over policy in this area, while stakeholders were unequivocal in their view that the EU's new competence in relation to sport was a positive development for both professional and grassroots sport. The UK is extremely well represented in EU Expert Groups on sport, providing the chair for three of them: Good Governance in Sport, Sustainable Financing of Sport, and Education and Training in Sport. All contributors who expressed a view felt that the current balance of competences in the field of sports was appropriate.

Assessment

Culture, tourism and sport are relatively new and secondary (niche) competences of the EU, particularly in the fields of culture and sports. All the contributors who submitted evidence held the view that the EU's current supporting competence in culture, tourism and sport was on balance either beneficial to the future development of these sectors and UK national interest or had the potential to be so. On the other hand, none of the contributors argued in favour of extending EU competences in these sectors, and advised vigilance over moves by the EU to extend these competences (p. 45).

The evidence at a glance – culture, tourism and sport

Niche competences appropriate and valuable for culture and sport

UK cultural organisations successful in securing EU funding

Important steps for free movement of footballers, and TV distribution

UK very well represented in sports governance bodies

---

6. External relations

6.1 *Foreign and security policy**

This Review examines the EU's foreign policy, or to use formal language its Common Foreign and Security Policy (CFSP), including Common Security and Defence Policy (CSDP). After giving an overview of Britain's foreign policy interests, the Review gives a richly documented account of the complex legal and institutional framework for the EU's foreign policy, its instruments and tools.

The Review does not go into the EU's external action under non-CFSP competences, which are covered in other, sector-specific Reviews (e.g. issues pertaining to trade and investment, EU enlargement, or the defence industry for that matter). The Review does cover civil protection, however, and the solidarity clause in the event of terrorist attacks or natural disasters, which fall outside of the scope of CFSP).

These editorial choices highlight important legal points. First, they underline the legal specificity of the CFSP. Indeed the CFSP is the only policy area covered explicitly in the Treaty on European Union (TEU) because it is "subject to specific rules and procedures" (Article 24(1), TEU), whereas all other competences are defined in the Treaty on the Functioning of the European Union (TFEU). The CFSP is an area characterised by the intergovernmental method of decision-making (largely by unanimity voting). The Review expresses this most vocally with respect to the CSDP): "each Member State has a power of veto, not least over the deployment of EU military operations and civilian missions. (…) The Member States can also act unilaterally, or via other international organisations, not least NATO, when they see fit (p.5)". Moreover, the roles of the Commission, the European Parliament and the Court of Justice remain limited in CFSP. In other words, the member states retain a high degree of sovereignty and control over the CFSP and CSDP. There are no powers to be repatriated here.

---

* Section contributed by Steven Blockmans.

Second, they expose problems related to competence delimitation between areas (CFSP and non-CFSP), which are governed by the different procedures and instruments. Whereas the EU's specific competences in the defence field (CSDP) are more or less clearly defined (Articles 42–46 TEU), the open-ended notion of "all areas of foreign policy and all questions relating to the Union's security" (Article 24(1) TEU) is rather unhelpful in determining the scope of CFSP. The sphere of the CFSP) does not extend to those external competences attributed to the Union under the TFEU (trade, financial and technical assistance, etc.). In the event of different interpretations among EU institutions and member states, it will eventually be up to the Court of Justice to settle the boundaries between CFSP/CSDP) and the other EU external policy domains. Such disputes are currently pending judgment before the Court.

Third, the CFSP) is a non-exclusive EU competence, since it runs concurrently with national competences in the same field. To make sure that the CFSP would not affect national competences, Declaration Nos. 13 and 14 to this effect were, upon the insistence of the UK,[22] attached to the Lisbon Treaty. In the same spirit the Review offers an *ex post* justification of the UK's controversial stance over 'representation creep' in the EU institutions' role in international organisations, which it is argued can lead to 'competence creep' (to use British political language). The criticism was made that High Representative Ashton was incrementally expanding her competence in external representation on behalf of the EU and its member states. For this reason, and much to the annoyance of the other 26 member states, in 2011 the UK held up the adoption of approximately 100 CFSP declarations, causing them to expire. The issue was supposedly resolved at the Council meeting of 22 October 2011 when there was endorsement of the "General Arrangements for EU Statements in multilateral organisations", although its content seems little more than a statement of the duty of sincere cooperation between EU institutions and member states (Articles 4(3) and 24(3) TEU).

---

[22] See House of Commons, Foreign Affairs Committee (2008) Foreign Affairs Policy Aspects of the Lisbon Treaty, Third Report of Session 2007-8, London, 16 January 2008.

Fourth, there is the need to reconcile such differences in order to enhance coherence in policy-making and the visibility and effectiveness of EU external action (writ large). This is illustrated with a set of case studies of prominent foreign policy issues in which the EU has been or is involved: the so-called strategic partnerships with China, Russia and the US; the Arab Spring; Iran's nuclear ambitions; human rights in Burma; restoring order in Mali; the stabilisation of Somalia; ensuring long-term stability in the Western Balkans; and rebuilding Afghanistan. These case studies show, in various ways, how the political, security and defence aspects of the EU's external action (led by the member states and External Action Service and decided by consensus in the Council) are increasingly interdependent with non-CFSP aspects of foreign policy, such as trade, energy, and transport relationships (which are largely led by the Commission and, in general, decided by qualified majority vote in the Council and majority vote in the EP).

Based on analysis of the evidence, the Review draws conclusions about the value added and the disadvantages for the UK of working through the EU in foreign policy. The key benefits include: "increased impact from acting in concert with 27 other countries; greater influence with non-EU powers, derived from [the UK's] position as a leading EU country; the international weight of the EU's single market, including its power to deliver commercially beneficial trade agreements; the reach and magnitude of EU financial instruments, such as for development and economic partnerships; the range and versatility of the EU's tools, as compared with other international organisations; and the EU's perceived political neutrality, which enables it to act in some cases where other countries or international organisations might not" (p.6).

The disadvantages of operating through the EU are: "challenges in formulating strong, clear strategy; uneven leadership; institutional divisions, and a complexity of funding instruments, which can impede implementation of policy; and sometimes slow or ineffective decision-making, due to complicated internal relationships and differing interests" (p.6).

Assessment

On foreign policy in general "the majority of correspondents argued that it is "strongly in the UK's interests to work through the EU" (p.87), (with the detailed arguments cited above). The disadvantages of slow and complicated decision-making (as cited above) are largely the result of the multiple and differentiated sets of competences and decision-making rules. The unanimity rule for all 'pure' foreign policy is in itself a major constraint, but this is often compounded by the need to join up with other EU competences that have external impacts.

On the other hand, the complexity of bringing together the EU's many external relations capabilities is also a reminder that the global governance challenges of the 21st century are profoundly changing the nature of foreign policy. The need for more effective global regulatory policies fits well with the broad development of the EU's own regulatory competences in recent decades. By contrast, in the hypothesis of UK secession from the EU, its residual national capabilities would (in the view of the present author) be thin and carry little weight by comparison. The view that secession by the UK would see a downgrading of its standing internationally has already been openly stated by the United States at the highest level, or as several commentators in the Review put it, the UK would be deprived of the EU serving as a 'force multiplier' for its foreign policy interests.

On defence, stakeholders were unanimous in the view that CSDP) operations could be improved, and that "most commentators" considered that this "came down to Member States' political will, both to deploy their personnel and invest in capabilities" (p.76), rather than a matter of institutions and legal competences.

The Review presents no proposals for changing EU competences in this domain. Effectiveness and efficiency are paramount objectives for whoever holds the competences, but simply to advocate better coordination and more political will seems to reflect more of a political preference to retain the status quo rather than to try to engineer solutions.

In its summary the Review says that it "suggested ways in which the EU could reform its external action to be more effective in playing its part" (p.7). While all can agree that there is room for qualitative improvement the Review is not so clear about how to do this, beyond saying that it is not a matter of changing legal competences. By contrast, 11 foreign ministers of the EU, including all the founding member states, issued a declaration in September 2012 favouring more majority voting in the foreign and defence fields.[23]

The evidence at a glance – foreign and security policy

Majority view, strongly in UK interest to work through the EU

EU as multiplier of UK interests

UK sovereignty guarded by unanimity rule and right to own national foreign policy; but disadvantage of slow decision-making

In global context, clear case to align EU international regulatory policies with foreign policy

Under secession hypothesis, the UK would carry little weight

6.2   *Development cooperation and humanitarian aid**

In both development cooperation and humanitarian aid the EU has 'parallel competences', meaning that it has competence to carry out activities and conduct a common policy, but that this does not prevent member states from exercising theirs (Article 4(4)TFEU). As a result there is nothing to repatriate in the sense of the member states regaining freedom of action for their own policies. The general view projected in the report is in support of this parallel competences regime. Critics make the case for improved implementation, not repatriation of competences.

Parallel policy-making at the EU level and at the national level, however, has the potential to result in conflicting policies. Member states have a tendency to 'upload' their development policies and objectives to the Union level, resulting in an EU

---

[23] Eleven EU foreign ministers, "Future of Europe" communiqué, 18 September 2012.

* Section contributed by Steven Blockmans.

development programme with an overloaded agenda, operating in almost every country in the world.

The EU and its member states account for about 60% of global Official Development Assistance (ODA). The Review acknowledges that the Commission's large aid budget provides economies of scale and strength in key areas such as infrastructure and regional projects. It leverages contributions from member states that might not otherwise commit equivalent funds to international development. Because EU aid is allocated over seven-year cycles, it provides a more predictable and longer-term source of finance than aid provided by donor countries (including the UK) or other organisations. The EU's global reach is much greater than that of any member state acting individually.

The EU is by far the UK's largest multilateral aid partner: £1.2 billion of UK aid was managed through the European Commission in 2011-12. Most of this aid (£812 million) is non-discretionary because it forms part of the UK's overall contribution to the EU general budget, which it is legally obliged to pay by virtue of being a member state. The rest is channelled through the European Development Fund (EDF), which is governed by the Cotonou Agreement. The UK spends the remainder of its aid budget bilaterally, working directly with 28 priority countries.

The fact that the EU is a major contributor to global efforts to reduce poverty; that it is perceived to be politically neutral; that it provides a platform for collective action and seeks to coordinate the efforts of its member states is seen by many respondents to be a major advantage of working through the EU. These attributes add value and have a multiplier effect on the UK's efforts to achieve its own policy objectives, as exemplified by the UK's role in negotiating the EU's 'Agenda for Change' programme of reform proposals for a more strategic EU approach to reducing poverty, including a more targeted allocation of funding.

The EU's competences in development cooperation and humanitarian aid link or overlap with related areas of EU competence in trade, neighbourhood relations, democracy and human rights, agriculture, fisheries, energy, environment, climate change and migration. This illustrates the richness of the EU's toolbox compared to other multilateral organisations, but also the challenges of coordination that this poses.

Since the introduction of the European External Action Service (EEAS) in 2011, responsibility for managing and disbursing EU aid has been split between the EEAS and two Directorates-General of the European Commission: that for Development and Cooperation (DEVCO), and that for Humanitarian Aid and Civil Protection (ECHO). In this collaborative framework, the Commission retains responsibility for developing policy proposals and for the overall management of the external instruments, whereas the EEAS contributes to the programming and management of these instruments. In doing so, the EEAS works with the Commission throughout the process and submits proposals to the Commission for adoption. The High Representative (and therefore the EEAS) is also tasked with ensuring the overall political coordination, as well as the unity, consistency and effectiveness of the EU's external actions and instruments. The report paints a fair picture of the well-documented difficulties that exist in finding the right working relationship between DG DEVCO and the EEAS, in particular.

These issues are well known in the member states themselves, which have experience of various models for the integration of development policy and management under foreign offices, or their separation. In the new EU system the argument has been made for DEVCO, and maybe also ECHO, to be integrated with the EEAS. Debate over these issues will doubtless continue. The division of roles between these two EU bodies is indeed far from simple.

The Review's biggest lament is that the EU development programme management and delivery is overly complex and inefficient. The checks built into the financial management systems (and the Financial Regulation in particular) have contributed to a common criticism of the Commission that it is overly bureaucratic. Commission rules are inflexible and cumbersome, which hamper project management's ability to achieve results; there is no clear overall system for demonstrating the results of EU-funded activities; and limited flexibility once funds have been committed to specific activities. This engenders the risk of steep falls in support once EU funding ends. The fact that the EU does not systematically measure the results that EU aid achieves is considered to be a major disadvantage.

Assessment

The 'parallel competence' regime or development cooperation is not challenged. Member states retain the freedom to run their own development policies, and there is no argument made that the EU should cease its activity in this field; on the contrary, the main argument is that the EU's programmes serve as a multiplier for UK (and other member states) policy objectives both in scale and range. The main criticism about efficiency leads into the well-known matter of cumbersome procedures at EU level, but here (in the opinion of the present author) the member states and European Parliament have to take their responsibilities for imposing on the Commission so many checks and constraints, which the Commission itself often considers to be excessive. The new institutional arrangements between the EEAS and the Commission (DEVCO and ECHO) remain the subject of uneasy concern, and may require revision in due course.

The evidence at a glance – development cooperation and humanitarian aid

Support for 'parallel competence', not limiting national competence

EU aid serves as multiplier of UK interests

Main criticism is over cumbersome procedures for EU aid

6.3   Enlargement*

As a subject of the first enlargement of the original European Communities, the UK continues to be a supporter of EU enlargement and the conditionality-based process of adaptation by candidates to the *acquis* (organised in 35 chapters, similar to the 32 Balance of Competence Reviews). As EU enlargement is, by its very nature, an issue that cuts across multiple policy areas, the evidence here links in with many other Reviews, but most topically regards the free movement of persons, on which more below.

---

* Section contributed by Steven Blockmans.

Enlargement policy cannot be categorised under the competence typology of Article 4 TFEU (exclusive, shared or supporting). Accession to the EU is achieved by way of a treaty between all member states and the applicant country, after following the procedure set out in the EU's membership clause of Article 49 TEU. This provision delineates the balance of competences between the member states and the EU institutions. It does not, however, spell out all eligibility conditions, nor does it codify the minutiae of the various stages in the pre-accession process. These details have been developed along the way.

In terms of the process, the member states in the (European) Council remain in control of every stage, from the definition of the membership criteria, to the direction of the enlargement strategy; whether to accept a membership application; to grant candidate country status; to open accession negotiations; to open individual negotiation chapters; to agree screening reports; to set opening/interim/closing benchmarks; or to conclude the negotiations, etc. The requirement of unanimity in decision-making means that, at each of these stages, individual member states may exercise a veto to block or hold up the progress of an aspirant country on its pre-accession track. Moreover, through their national ratification procedures for accession treaties, each national parliament also has a veto on new members joining the EU. There is therefore no 'repatriation' question here.

The report shows that there is hardly any support for a change in this balance of competences, even if unanimity has at times worked against UK interests, with some other member states blocking or upholding accession negotiations (such as Greece in the case of Macedonia and France in the case of Turkey). British stakeholders generally believe that member states and the EU institutions have been effective in managing the enlargement process, and in learning and implementing lessons from previous accession waves. They note how the UK has been at the forefront of driving these reforms. Moreover, the EU institutions have continued to function satisfactorily in the wake of successive enlargement rounds, in spite of earlier concerns about gridlock in decision-making.

Much of the evidence in the Review focuses on the use of pre-accession conditionality. Stakeholders generally support the increasing emphasis placed by the EU on overcoming bilateral disputes, improving regional cooperation, and ensuring the implementation of reforms. There is also support for the Commission's more recent move to 'front-load' requirements for the rule of law (including fighting organised crime and corruption), public administration reform, and economic governance and competitiveness, which is an approach advocated by the UK and like-minded member states.

Most contributors believe that the enlargement process has generally worked well in ensuring that candidate countries transpose the EU's *acquis* in full. There is, however, awareness that the EU's conditionality has been less effective in ensuring post-accession compliance with the political accession criteria and the EU's values (as in the cases of Hungary, Bulgaria and Romania). Some contributors made the point that the enlargement process has not yet been able to overcome more daunting political obstacles, such as in the cases of Bosnia and Herzegovina, Macedonia and Turkey.

With regard to the impact of enlargement on UK interests, the evidence suggests that, while there have been undesirable effects in some areas, the EU's widening has been and is likely to continue to be seen as generally beneficial to the UK. Contributors point out that the UK has enjoyed significant influence among new and aspirant member states as a result of promoting EU enlargement. The Review notes that many contributors believe that the enlarged EU has become a more comfortable environment for the UK, with the accession of many countries that share its liberal trading and Atlanticist outlook, and have a preference for English as a working language. Many contributors feel that the UK has benefited from a larger EU, more able – as an 'influence-multiplier' – to deal on equal terms with other world powers, notably in negotiations on trade. A great majority of contributors agree that British business has benefited from access to an enlarged single market of more than 500 million consumers. However, some evidence suggests that British SMEs have not yet fully exploited opportunities in new member states.

Some contributors suggest that enlargement, by lowering barriers, may have made it easier for international crime to reach the UK. Others believe that widening the EU has in fact extended the reach of law enforcement and judicial cooperation across the continent, thus strengthening the UK's external defences against organised crime and terrorism.

The UK government points out that enlargement can have deleterious consequences in some areas, with growing cross-party agreement that the impact on migratory flows to the UK should be addressed. The UK was among the few member states willing to remove all restrictions on free movement from the moment of the 'big bang' accession of new member states in 2004, whereas many other member states insisted on transitional regimes. As a result, the UK experienced a particularly large spike in immigration, which has now pushed it into the more restrictive camp. Prime Minister Cameron has called for reform of the temporary post-accession controls on free movement, in order to ensure continued public confidence in and support for the process. He suggests that achievement of a certain level of GDP per capita in relation to the EU average should be used as a condition for removing all transitional restrictions on free movement.

Assessment

Enlargement has been dubbed the EU's most successful foreign policy, having contributed crucially to the democratic and economic transformation of Central and Eastern Europe.

Enlargement has also fitted with the UK's vision of a wider, looser, more flexible Europe. It is perceived as benefiting the UK because, inter alia, it increases the number of member states not (yet) in the eurozone, thus reducing the risk of Britain's isolation.

Given the leading role of the member states on EU enlargement, it comes as no surprise that the Review produces no case for changing the current balance of competences in this area. On the contrary, there seems to be evidence of some 'creeping nationalisation' in the process, with each member state able to use its veto power to protect its interests.[24] The Review even suggests

---

[24] Christophe Hillion, "The Creeping Nationalisation of the EU Enlargement Policy", SIEPS Report No. 6, November 2010.

that individual capitals may at times have abused the enlargement process to extract bilateral concessions from candidate countries. This has consequences for the EU's credibility and ability to exercise leverage to promote reforms. Moreover, such practices undermine the mandate given to the Commission to run the day-to-day process on behalf of the Council in the EU's collective interest.

A key theme emerging from the evidence is that, unless public confidence can be maintained, enlargement is at risk of grinding to a halt, with the issue of immigration from newly acceding EU member states having risen to the top of the agenda in the UK, and to a lesser degree in some other member states. This has cast a shadow over enlargement policy for the future. How to phase in free movement is certainly an issue for ongoing or new negotiations with candidate countries. It is difficult to predict when and where serious problems may arise in the future, however. The very recent Croatian accession saw no marked influx of migrants, for example, and the next most plausible accession candidates, Serbia and Montenegro, are unlikely to do so either. Bigger issues would no doubt arise with a populous country such as Turkey, whose GDP per capita has been rising in relation to the EU average, but whose accession is not yet on the political horizon. The unanimity rules governing the accession process leave all member states with full powers to control the process.

The evidence at a glance – enlargement

No competence question, member states control accession process at every stage

Crucial achievements in democratic transformation of Central and Eastern Europe

UK traditionally a strong supporter of EU enlargement

Suits UK interests in a liberal Atlanticist Europe

More non-eurozone countries (for the time being) reduces risks of isolation

Recent stiffening of UK position on immigration from new member states: a matter for negotiation if a new accession candidate threatens large-scale migration

7. General issues

7.1 Voting, consular services and statistics

This is a mixed bag of important issues. The overall pattern of evidence is that current arrangements are broadly satisfactory. While there are demands for reforms that go further than what the British government would support, there are no prospects of major pressure for such changes.

Voting

From 2002 it was decided that there should be a uniform electoral process in elections for the European Parliament, based on common principles. This requires a proportional representation system, but with an open choice to be made between a list versus a single transferable vote system. For the UK this meant a move away from its established single-member constituency system for the House of Commons. This innovation seems to have passed into effect without notable objections.

In March 2013 the Commission published a non-binding recommendation that there be a common voting day, given that while most member states vote on Sunday, a few vote on Thursday (including the UK), Friday or Saturday. The Review records the British government's view that this traditional voting day should not be changed. While many people may feel this to be an uninteresting matter to defend, there has been no forcing of the issue, and Thursday voting remains intact.

One issue discussed was whether EU citizens resident in a member state other than their own should be able to vote in national elections, but this would require the unanimous agreement of member states. The UK government considers that the status quo, with such EU citizens able to vote in local and European Parliament elections only, strikes the right balance.

The Review discusses various theoretical options for the future of the European Parliament, including having a second chamber made up of national MPs. But there was no strong evidence to support changing the status quo here either.

Overall, the evidence suggested that there was no need for significant reform of the present balance of competences in this field.

Consular Services

The main EU provision regarding consular services concerns assistance to 'unrepresented EU citizens', i.e. EU nationals requiring assistance in a foreign country where their own government was not represented. A Council Decision of 1995 requires that such assistance should be provided on a non-discriminatory basis. The evidence received suggested that this was the appropriate level of EU competence. The European External Action Service is not equipped to deliver consular assistance, but may play a useful coordinating role, especially in crisis situations.

However, there is discussion on how consular services should be provided in the future, especially for those many smaller member states that do not have the virtually global cover of consular services enjoyed by France, Germany and the UK. There is already a move towards co-location, with the UK having 14 locations co-located with other EU or Commonwealth countries, and a further 20 locations being prepared for similar arrangements.

The more radical option would be to establish 'European consulates', an idea the European Commission has circulated since 2006. In the long run such offices could issue visas and legalise documents. EU High Representative Baroness Ashton reported to the Council in 2011 that a number of member states favoured the EU Delegations developing such functions, whereas others, including the UK, were opposed to such developments. Within the Schengen area there is already a trend towards an increasing number of shared visa processing offices hosted in the consulate of a single member state, from which the UK stands aside, for obvious reasons.

There seems to be no imminent change in present arrangements, although the combination of rising demand for consular services and increasingly severe budgetary constraints may lead to more important developments towards common consular services in due course.

Statistics

There is no doubt about the essential importance of comparable statistics for sound policy-making at both national and EU levels. Among examples cited in the Review, strictly comparable data on gross national income are the basis for budgetary contributions to the EU, and more broadly the harmonised system of national accounts are vital to economic policy surveillance. Energy, environment and climate change policies depend on sound data. Almost every line of policy-making has similar needs.

Data collection costs are considerable, and there is a clear trade-off between the substantial benefits of comparability and assured quality of UK and European statistics on the one hand, and the potential burden on UK respondents and costs to UK statistical producers on the other. The Review reports that "the balance of the evidence received indicates that the current competence results in a broadly acceptable trade-off for UK interests" (p.117).

One noted concern is the Intrastat system for collecting data on trade internal to the EU. This has to be collected through surveys of firms, since intra-EU customs controls have been scrapped, and this source of data only exists now for the EU's external trade. The Intrastat system involves threshold levels of trade that require reporting. There is general recognition of the need to reform Intrastat, with the Council calling for "a substantial reduction in the response burden…, while maintaining a sound level of quality…" (p.112). While these are no doubt laudable objectives, it should be remembered that the costs of the Intrastat system have to be compared with the much higher costs of the paperwork and delays of former customs procedures that were abolished though completion of the single market.

Another reform objective is to improve the basic statistics Regulation (223/2009) in order to make the system more robust and independent of political pressures. This follows the serious problem of fraudulent statistics uncovered in the case of Greece when basic national accounts data were found to have been manipulated in 2004 for purposes related to the monitoring of economic policy within the eurozone. While this case is an extreme one, the general issue of optimal independence of statistics producers is an ongoing debate, with the proposed new regulation not yet adopted because of differences of view on this point between the European Parliament and Commission.

The evidence at a glance – voting, consular services, statistics

Voting

Present competences considered satisfactory

UK accepted proportional representation for European Parliament elections

Proposal for common voting day not supported by UK, and not pursued

Discussion of question of voting rights of EU citizens in national elections of 'other' member states, but no consensus for change

Consular services

Main current arrangement is for consular assistance for 'unrepresented EU citizens' on a non-discriminatory basis

Budgetary pressures lead to co-location of consulates, which the UK does increasingly

Longer-term case for 'Europe consulates' has support of some member states, but opposition from others

Statistics

Need for comparable statistics generally recognised to aid sound policy-making

Reforms desired to minimise reporting burdens, but current competence broadly acceptable

---

7.2 Subsidiarity and proportionality (S & P)

This Review, about whether and how far the EU should act, structures the arguments according to a logical framework of three, tiered principles:

- First, the principle of conferral, i.e. whether the EU has the legal competence to act in a certain area of policy;

- Second, the principle of subsidiarity. Thus "subsidiarity is not a type competence, but rather a principle that must be followed by the EU when considering whether or not to exercise competence" (p.18);

- Third, the principle of proportionality, i.e. whether, when an action is justified, the EU acts with due regard to avoid unnecessary burdensome regulations.

The principle of subsidiarity has seen a steady increase in its standing in the EU's legal and operational order over the last three decades. Subsidiarity was first introduced, but only implicitly, into the EU's legal order with the Single European Act of 1987, but then reinforced explicitly in the Treaty of Maastricht in 1993. In the Treaty of Amsterdam of 1999 there followed a Protocol (No 20) that further defined how the principles of both subsidiarity and proportionality should be applied. Finally, in 2007 the Lisbon Treaty (in Protocol No 2) enhanced the role of national parliaments in controlling the application in practice of the subsidiarity principle, introducing the so-called 'yellow card' and 'orange card' procedures. The 'yellow card' provides that one-third of national parliaments can require a legislative proposal to be reviewed, while the 'orange card' provides that a simple majority of national parliaments may impose more onerous conditions on the Commission to proceed with a contested proposal. The yellow card procedure has been used twice, but the orange card has not yet been used. In addition, the Lisbon Treaty introduced provisions for national parliaments to take a case to the European Court of Justice (CJEU) where legislation is deemed to breach the principle of subsidiarity.

Proportionality has been described "as an expression of simple common sense - don't use a sledgehammer to crack a nut" (p.34). Its origins go back a long way before the EU's existence and has broadly been seen as "the need to protect individuals from the coercive power of the state" (p.34). In the EU context the principle of proportionality as a matter of EU law has developed primarily through the case law of the European Court of Justice. For example in 2005 in the ABNA case the CJEU struck down an EU directive requiring manufacturers of animal feed to indicate the exact composition of the feed, on the grounds that this went beyond what was required to protect human health (p.37). One consequence of CJEU case law on proportionality is a rising number of instances where national rules may be challenged for being disproportionate, as in the seminal *Cassis de Dijon* (Case 120/78) of 1979. This is an important perspective in the political debate about proportionality, where the CJEU can strike down disproportionate national as well as EU practices (p.38).

The Review devotes a section to the related but separate issue of the use of the 'catch-all' Article 352 as legal basis for EU action in cases where no specific legal basis is available. The concern here is that the Article 352 purpose of adding flexibility to the EU's legal processes could be abused to expand the EU's effective competences beyond those authorised explicitly in the treaties. The Review notes that this article has been little used, given the breadth of competences defined now in the Lisbon Treaty, and restrictions placed upon its use (p.43).

The Review sensibly took the trouble to screen for evidence on S & P issues in the many sectoral policy Reviews, and quoted examples of issues arising in the fields of agriculture, animal health and welfare, fisheries, energy, environment, transport, competition policy, financial services, social and employment policies and fundamental rights (pp. 55-57, pp. 75-78, and in more detail pp. 110-115).

Examples of where there were complaints that S & P principles were being inadequately respected include land use planning and noise, recreational transport (aviation, rail), rules for driving licenses, animal health standards adapted to the UK's island geography. Another example is where the CJEU had ruled against flexibility for member states to adopt lighter reporting requirements on health and safety issues for businesses employing fewer than 11 people. Cases often cited in the UK debate are the Directives on Working Time and Agency Workers.

Going in the other direction, there were several cases cited where the processes of negotiation and consultation led to corrections to respond to S & P complaints, including reforms in fisheries policy allowing for regional groupings (North Sea, Mediterranean), the recent agreement on energy-climate policies to allow for differentiated national implementation of EU-agreed targets, and in the case of the Data Protection Regulation the elimination of many provisions allowing for detailed powers to be delegated to the Commission.

Assessment

The most frequent critique in the Review is over the need to improve the quality of impact assessments and to ensure more time and greater transparency in consultation processes. Related issues are the need to ensure better regulatory quality and cut unnecessary 'red tape'. The British[25] and Dutch[26] governments have produced lists of regulations that could be scrapped or lightened. The British government welcomes the Commission's ongoing work through its 'Regulatory Fitness and Performance Programme (REFIT)',[27] which reports regularly on regulations that should be improved or repealed.

The Review pays close detailed attention to the case for national parliaments to develop a more effective role in controlling for S & P issues. Debate on this issue is widespread among member states, and the UK's concerns are shared by many others. Detailed proposals are discussed, for example whether the 'yellow card' procedures should be seriously upgraded into 'red card' procedures, where a majority of national parliaments could play a more decisive role in blocking legislation on S & P grounds. These are delicate matters that do not invite simple conclusions, given the need to enhance the perceived democratic legitimacy of the EU at national levels, but also to avoid constitutional confusion of responsibilities between the governments of member states in the Council and their national parliaments.

The Review takes note of the innovation seen in the incoming Commission on 1 November 2014, in the new position of a First Vice-President (former Dutch Minister of Foreign Affairs, Frans Timmermans) charged explicitly with controlling for respect

---

[25] "Cut EU red tape", Report from the Business Taskforce (commissioned by the British Prime Minister), October 2013.

[26] "Testing European legislation for subsidiarity and proportionality – Dutch list of points for action", June 2013 (www.government.nl/documents-and-publications/notes/2013/06/21/testing-european-legislation-for-subsidiarity-and-proportionality-dutch-list-of-points-for-action.html).

[27] European Commission, "Regulatory Fitness and Performance Programme (REFIT)", COM(2014) 368 final, 18.6.2014.

of subsidiarity and proportionality in any legislative proposals to come out of the Commission. "This suggests that there will be a firmer focus on these issues within the 2014-2019 Commission, and the opportunity for greater engagement with the concerns and proposals of Member States and national parliaments" (p.99).

To conclude, the evidence is that the principles of subsidiarity and proportionality are being taken increasingly seriously among member states and EU institutions. This is a logical political response to the growth of EU competences that has occurred over the last three decades. The above-mentioned institutional innovation in the Commission adds to the build-up of treaty-level safeguards against EU policies that contravene these principles. The UK is well placed to build coalitions in favour of the broader quest for regulatory quality, notably because its government and stakeholders work hard on these difficult and often very detailed technical matters.

The evidence at a glance – subsidiarity and proportionality (S & P)

Continuous build-up of S & P principles in the law and practices of the EU, alongside the build-up of EU competences and increased qualified majority voting in the Council

Complaints over insufficient respect for S & P in several sectors, but evidence of the processes of consultation and negotiation leading to corrections

Widespread calls for improved impact assessments and more time and transparency for consultations

Ongoing debate on how to enhance the role of national parliaments

Ongoing debate on how to cut 'red tape'

New appointment of First Vice-President of the Commission to control proposals for S & P, signalling that processes may be reformed to become more rigorous

---

PART III – CONCLUSIONS

1. By groups of policies

In the conclusions that follow we consolidate the broad findings of the Reviews by groups of policy. Key points from the evidence are summarised in Table 1.

For the *core single market policies*, namely the four freedoms plus competition and external trade policies, there is generally strong UK support for the EU's competences, except for reservations over the free movement of people. While the UK unequivocally backs the single market only for goods, services and capital, the rest of the EU insists that the integrity of all four freedoms together is fundamental and an untouchable red line (on which more below).

All four freedoms demonstrate importantly different characteristics. For the free movement of goods the EU system has in effect reached a state of maturity, following substantial reform measures adopted in the 1990s to lighten the harmonisation process in favour of a high degree of mutual recognition, under the leadership of the British Commissioner at that time, Lord Cockfield. For the free movement of services the system is still far from complete, and the UK is at the forefront of those pushing for stronger effective EU measures to eliminate contradictory national regulations, so here the reform agenda remains very much open. For financial markets there has been a continuing process of drastic reform in the wake of the 2008 financial crisis, starting with the de Larosière report, which set the reforms off to a remarkably fast start, and remain ongoing. The UK's City interests have so far been adequately protected, which would cease to be the case in the event of secession.

Table 1. Summary of Balance of Competence findings

Sector of policy	Competence question
Core single market policies	
Single market overview	Strategic priority for UK. Widespread support for EU competence.
Free movement of goods	Key 1992 reform: mutual recognition & less harmonisation.
Free movement of services	UK interests in enhanced EU policy, including digital sector.
Free movement of capital	Major reforms since the 2008 crisis. UK City interests protected.
Free movement of persons	Benefits and costs contested within UK. Curbs proposed (not crossing EU red line?)
Competition/consumer policy	Competition policy strongly supported, consumer policy nuance.
External trade & investment	EU competence vital. No good alternatives outside EU.
Sectoral policies	
Transport	EU competence supported, UK leading role in shaping policy.
Agriculture	Severely criticised, but policy gradually reformed over decades.
Fisheries	Severely criticised, but radical reforms achieved in 2013
Energy	UK increasing energy importer, driver for enhanced EU policy.
Environment & climate	UK driver of EU policies. EU as amplifier of UK interests.
Food safety, animal welfare	EU harmonised approach essential, UK a driver of EU policies.
Public health	Limited EU actions useful, including inflow of health professionals.
Digital information rights	EU competence necessary, UK active in defining rapidly evolving priorities.
Economic, monetary, social policies	
Economic and monetary union	UK opt-out of both euro currency and coercive aspects of fiscal policy coordination
Social & employment	Divisive issue in UK. Controversy over a few directives.

Taxation	Limited EU competences useful. Unanimity rule safeguards.
EU budget	UK retains special rebate; achieves reform with real cuts for future.
Cohesion	Competence for some regional solidarity supported.
Justice and home affairs	
Fundamental rights	Divisive UK debate over European Court of Human Rights (i.e. Strasbourg, not EU).
Civil justice	UK opt-outs & opt-back-ins, flexibility suiting UK legal system
Police and criminal justice	UK opt-outs & opt-back-ins, flexibility suiting UK legal system.
Asylum, non-EU immigration	UK opt-out of Schengen, and selective opt-in arrangements on asylum.
Education, research, culture	
Education	'Erasmus generation' a transformative achievement.
Research & space	UK major beneficiary of EU projects; big science achievements.
Tourism, culture & sport	EU niche activities useful; UK driver for sports governance.
External relations	
Foreign policy	EU multiplier of UK interests. Unanimity rule safeguard.
Development & humanitarian aid	EU multiplier of UK interests. UK free to set own aid policy.
Consular services	Budgetary pressures for rationalisation.
Enlargement	Member states control whole process with unanimity grip; UK traditional supporter.
General	
Voting, statistics	Present competences satisfactory.
Subsidiarity & proportionality	New Commission appointment signals increasing priority.

There is a large group of *sectoral policies* that are buttressing the single market, as well as pursuing their own specific policy objectives. These are all 'shared' competences, and the evidence shows that the detailed sharing between EU and national legislation is in most cases found to be broadly appropriate. This also fits with perceptions of the UK's national interests, both in government and business circles. Several important sectors stand out as being of particular interest to the UK, notably energy, environment and climate change, financial markets, transport, the digital sector, and services in general. In all these sectors UK ministers and senior officials have played leading roles in shaping or reforming the EU policies in question. The evidence here is that the EU's competences at the level at which they are defined in the treaties are not only uncontested; on the contrary it is widely considered – in both the UK and the EU as a whole – that stronger EU policies in these sectors are necessary.

On the free movement of people, the arguments played out in current British political debate, in our opinion, need a sense of proportion, for three reasons. First, the evidence shows how immigration from the EU helps fill gaps in the labour market, with various striking examples such as the contribution of nurses and other health professionals from the EU to the functioning of the National Health Service, and to the UK building and construction sectors that are hard pressed to find the workers they need.

Second, as regards tensions in society over problems of multiculturalism, the greatest concerns arise in non-EU immigrant communities, in particular those that have seen the radicalisation of young Muslims, with several hundred young British Muslims enrolling as 'foreign fighters' with ISIS in Syria. In the wake of the colossal *Charlie Hebdo* tragedy in Paris in January 2015 the common priority of European leaders is enhanced cooperation over security; by comparison problems associated with intra-EU migration, such as the capacity of schools to handle increasing enrolments, are of a second order.

Third, as regards EU policies, the freedom of movement for people concerns the right to circulate and take up employment, and does not include the right to reside or to receive comprehensive welfare benefits on a non-contributory basis, as has recently been confirmed by the European Court of Justice.[28] This ruling does not support the stereotypical argument that the Court is an agent of EU 'competence creep' since this decision clearly upholds national competences. Member states thus retain competence for determining the right to residence and thence details of what social security benefits can be extended to immigrants from other EU member states. The UK is not alone in wanting to tighten up on these national policies, which can be done without calling into question basic EU legal competences. Prime Minister Cameron set out his agenda on 28 November 2014 for further tightening the system to limit immigration without, however, breaching the cardinal rule of free movement of persons. It will take some time to clarify the extent to which these proposals can be implemented on the basis of existing national competences, or how far they will require more or less difficult negotiations with the rest of the EU.

The broad single market sector, the four freedoms and sectoral policies make up a large proportion of EU legislation. The hypothetical alternative of national competences, for example for product safety and the prudential regulation of service sectors, is not a plausible prospect. National regulations would not necessarily be less demanding, but would have the serious drawback of allowing 28 variations that would effectively disintegrate the single market and permit reintroduction of protectionist technical barriers to trade. To be sure, there is debate about whether the EU produces too much red tape, to which we return below under the *reform* agenda.

The broad domain of *economic, monetary and social policies* presents a much more varied story. The biggest issue here is the eurozone system, which has undergone huge crises and systemic developments since 2008. The eurozone system proved defective, and the response has been to reinforce eurozone-level competences with the setting up of the banking union and massively increased financial assistance to sovereign debtors in difficulty. There have also been reinforcements of the procedures and powers at

---

[28] Dano case, C-333/13, 11 November.

European level to constrain budget deficits, which remains a highly contested matter. Yet this does not directly affect the British situation, since it has a permanent opt-out from the euro system, and the UK has been able to use its own macroeconomic and monetary powers to recover faster from the recession than the eurozone. In fact, the UK might be described as having been able to take a 'free ride' on the eurozone. More precisely, soon after the financial crisis of 2008 the UK saw a 20% devaluation of the pound against the euro which, combined with continued full access to the single market, may have helped it get back onto a positive growth path ahead of the eurozone. In the hypothetical absence of the eurozone there would have been a chaotic movement of intra-European exchange rates, with the UK unable to bank upon a simple devaluation against the rest of the EU.

Of other items in this group of policies, the Review on *taxation* notes the EU's limited but useful competences, and the safeguard that exists against 'competence creep', since all measures on taxation require unanimity.

On the *EU budget* there are two features of special relevance to the UK. The first is that over the years the UK has renegotiated the initially weak corrective mechanism adopted before the 1975 referendum, and since Margaret Thatcher's premiership a substantial rebate mechanism has been in place, which is guarded by its treaty status (i.e. it can only be changed by unanimous decision, and therefore with UK acquiescence). The second is that the UK negotiated hard to secure a reduction in real terms in the new 2014-20 multiannual commitments for the EU budget, which Prime Minister Cameron has marked up as an important reform.

In the case of the *cohesion (or regional) policy* the case is made in the Review to restrict funding to poorer member states only, thus repatriating the competence for richer member states. This proposition has a rationale, but is not at present generally accepted by other richer member states, or by Scotland, Wales or Northern Ireland.

As for *social and employment policies*, the UK has followed a zigzag path, opting out of the Social Chapter at the time of the Maastricht Treaty in 1992, opting in with the Amsterdam Treaty in 1997 with the Labour government, but resuming criticism of some pieces of labour market legislation under the present government.

In the field of *freedom, security and justice* the picture is dominated by opt-outs for the UK and Ireland, not only for the Schengen system of border control and visa policies, but also judicial and police cooperation in interior ministry affairs. The UK has managed to secure the agreement of the rest of the EU to have huge flexibility in choosing where it wants to opt back in to selective provisions of EU law. No other member state, except Ireland, is able to do this, and no accession candidate could possibly secure such terms. The rest of the EU is on a determined course to reinforce EU policies in the broad justice and home affairs domain, but the UK can stand aside from these except where it wants to join in, subject to the agreement of the rest of the EU. In the field of civil judicial cooperation the UK again has an opt-out, with the possibility to pick and choose in accordance with its perception of what fits sufficiently well with British legal tradition.

The UK's threat to withdraw from the European Convention on Human Rights and the European Court of Human Rights in Strasbourg, while not directly a matter for the EU, would undermine the cause of human rights in wider Europe.

The *education and research* nexus of policies sees clear successes for British interests in the EU, supporting its world-class university system and research capabilities. The UK attracts a high number of students to its universities from the rest of the EU under the Erasmus programme, and wins more competitive EU-funded research contracts than any other member state except Germany. For some of the EU's relatively minor competences, such as for aspects of *public health, culture and international sport*, the findings are that the EU is performing a valuable supporting role, without challenging the major responsibilities of the member states in any way.

The evolution of EU *foreign and security policies* is broadly seen as a 'force multiplier' for UK interests and values, with the wish expressed for it to become more effective. At the same time the unanimity rule for decision-making guards against UK concerns about 'competence creep'.

The evidence at a glance – by sector

UK key interest in deepening broad single market domain

UK driver of policy development in many sectors (external trade, services, energy, climate, environment, food safety, digital)

Several other sectors clearly beneficial for UK (research, education, public health)

On immigration from EU, national action can control for 'benefit tourism' without challenging free movement

Foreign & development aid policies as 'multipliers' of UK interests

Major opt-outs where policies not in UK interests (euro, Schengen), etc.)

2. By reform, renegotiation, or repatriation

As regards the three stated categories of possible action - reform, renegotiation, and repatriation – the following conclusions emerge.

Reform. The reform agenda – past, present and future – is shown by the Reviews to be extensive in virtually all areas of policy. In justifying his switch of position on the EU to advocacy of secession in 2013, Lord Lawson declared that the EU was "unreformable"; a position also adopted by the spokesmen of the UKIP party.[29] This does not fit with the evidence, however. Maybe even more surprising for British public opinion: the evidence shows that UK negotiators in EU affairs, both at political and senior official levels, have a remarkable track record of leading policy reform or improvement across many sectors. The serious problems for the UK in agricultural policy mainly arose because the ground rules were negotiated before the UK's accession. By contrast, the UK's policy influence since accession in 1973 has been very substantial, comparing favourably with any other member state. This is illustrated in several sectors, including cases where the UK and others see the need for enhanced and not diminished EU policies, such as energy, climate change, service sectors, financial services, the digital sector, among others. A notable past example was in the early 1990s when the single market was

---

[29] "It's Time to Quit", *The Times*, 7 May 2013.

advanced by adoption of seminal concepts such as 'mutual recognition', which lessened the burden of harmonising regulations.

Two notoriously controversial sectors, *agriculture and fisheries*, have undergone significant reform along lines advocated by the UK. Reform of agricultural policy proves to be a decades-long process, and one that has to go on. The 'butter mountains' are no more, however. This represents reforms achieved since the 1990s from production support to income support. The burden for the EU budget remains considerable, but has nonetheless declined from its 75% share of the total in 1985 to the 36% planned for 2014-2020. For fisheries the reforms decided in 2013 are a sharper and more immediately effective correction of past problems, represented most clearly in public opinion by the anomalous policy of 'discards' of fish back into the sea, which has now stopped alongside other more basic reform measures.

On another source of British discontent: certain *labour market and social policies* see an increasing trend towards 'soft law', i.e. non-binding peer pressure such as in the Lisbon Strategy for 2000-2010, followed by the Europe 2020 programme for the following decade. Here the reform agenda has increasingly followed British ideas favouring a flexible labour market, or concepts of 'flexicurity' (i.e. combinations of flexibility and security; a term first advocated by the Danish Prime Minister).

There remains the live debate about whether the EU is managing its regulatory work and responsibilities as efficiently as it might, or whether it is producing too much red tape. For an independent view on this question the Commission invited Edmund Stoiber, Prime Minister of Bavaria, to chair a High Level Group to advise it on how to reduce regulatory burdens.[30] This

---

[30] High Level Group on Administrative Burdens (chaired by Edmund Stoiber, former Prime Minister of Bavaria), "Cutting Red Tape in Europe – Legacy and Outlook", Final Report, 24 July 2014. The main report is available at: http://ec.europa.eu/smart-regulation/refit/admin_burden/docs/08-10web_ce-brocuttingredtape_en.pdf.

Full information on the work of the group and annexes to the final report are available at: http://ec.europa.eu/smartregulation/refit/admin_burden/high_level_group_en.htm

report made various recommendations, including for setting a net target to reduce regulatory costs, for a 'one-in one-out' constraint on setting new business regulations, and to exempt small and micro businesses "where appropriate" from various regulations. While these kinds of overarching proposals may be attractive politically they risk (in our opinion) proving too simplistic to be operational, and cannot dispense from the hard grind of assessing the details of masses of legislation item by item.

The Stoiber report commented positively on current developments as follows: "With the new approach of Smart Regulation and the launch of the REFIT Programme, President Barroso and the Commission as a whole have initiated a fundamental change in the EU law-making process. I believe that this re-direction, which has led to a change of working methods within the Commission, is a real quantum leap". While this comment may be a little on the over-optimistic side, there is little doubt that the campaign to cut Brussels red tape is gaining traction.

In particular, the new Juncker Commission, starting in November 2014, charged its First Vice-President explicitly with controlling respect for the principles of subsidiarity and proportionality.

This will give a boost to the Commission's ongoing work under the REFIT heading (Regulatory Fitness and Performance Programme), which aims at a simple, clear and predictable regulatory framework, to simplify legislation so that the policy objectives are achieved at the lowest cost and with respect for the principles of subsidiarity and proportionality.[31] Under REFIT, the Commission is screening the entire stock of EU legislation on an ongoing and systematic basis to identify burdens, inconsistencies and ineffective measures and to set out corrective actions. Its current work programme identifies a dozen priorities (listed in Box 2). These are mostly small items, and irritants more than

---

[31] European Commission, "Regulatory Fitness and Performance Programme *(REFIT):* State of Play and Outlook", COM(2014) 368 final, 18.6.2014.

anything else, but to weed them out responds to widespread popular demand.

Box 2. Administrative Burden Reduction Plus Programme (ABR+): priority simplifications

- Simplified accounting/auditing for SMEs
- Exempt micro enterprises from accounting directives
- Simplifying notification system for shipments of waste
- Limitation of documents procurement procedures
- Fewer respondents for statistics on intra-EU trade
- Reduced reporting on industrial production
- Lesser requirements for electronic invoicing
- Reduce foreign language burdens for VAT refunds
- Exemptions from tachograph rules for SMEs
- Fewer 'documents on board' in transport sector
- Simplified egg labelling

Source: European Commission, op. cit.

For perspective, the complaints about the burdens of EU regulations have to be assessed alongside the more general issue of red tape originating at national as well as EU levels. It should be recalled that whenever there is a food safety crisis, such as in the horsemeat scandal of 2013, the conclusion tends to be that national implementation of EU regulations needs to be reinforced, and not that EU regulations should be abandoned. Even more dramatically, the financial crisis of 2008 demonstrated the grave inadequacy of national regulatory policies in this area.

A related complaint heard in public debate is that the EU accounts for an excessively large share of legislation adopted by national parliaments, and figures like 75% are sometimes loosely spoken of without identified sources. The House of Commons has conducted a thorough study on this point, however.[32] This is a difficult statistical matter, since single acts of legislation can range in importance from the state budget to technical regulations about

---

[32] "How much legislation comes from Europe?", House of Commons Library, Research Paper 10/62, 13 October 2010.

the labelling of foods, and much EU legislation is in this second category. Subject to these important qualifications the House of Commons study concluded: "In the UK data suggest that from 1997 to 2009 6.7% of primary legislation (Statutes) and 14.1% of secondary legislation (Statutory Instruments) has a role in implementing EU obligations, although the degree of involvement varied from passing reference to explicit implementation". The study also shows how there was a high peak in EU-based legislation during the 1980s and early 1990s when the single market was being completed, and since then the numbers have declined by two-thirds.

The heaviness or lightness of touch of regulatory systems varies greatly between EU member states, and the UK is often at the lighter end of this spectrum. The EU's regulations in the employment and social policy field have not prevented the UK from having one of the most liberal labour markets, as does Denmark, which is at the top of world rankings for the quality of its economic and human development. By contrast, Belgium and France are among the member states whose labour markets are regulated in the most burdensome manner. Data illustrating these divergences are provided by the World Bank's 'ease of doing business' rankings.[33] Broadly speaking, the member states are grouped in three categories, most of Northern Europe with high rankings for 'ease of doing business', France, Spain and Belgium in second category of much less 'ease', with Italy and Greece coming in a third category (alongside Belarus and Russia).

Of the countries mentioned above, those in the top and middle categories are all law-abiding member states, implementing the same EU laws seriously. Yet the economic impacts of their overall regulatory regimes are quite different, as the small example of three architectural practices in Box 4 vividly illustrates with regard to the cases of Britain, Belgium and France.

---

[33] www.doingbusiness.org/rankings, World Bank, June 2014.

Box 3. A cosmopolitan London narrative

A young boutique architectural practice in London, specialising in projects of high artistic value, employs 28 architects, of whom one-third are British, with nine other EU nationalities making up the rest, together with three 'tech-savvy' Asians. Average age, early thirties. The British founders of the company recently met a couple of their professional counterparts in Paris and Brussels. While their London practice has grown rapidly, Paris and Brussels remain stuck at around five architects. Why did London grow, when Paris and Brussels did not? The London office grew because it could tap into the entire European labour market for highly skilled and specialised young architects with zero bureaucracy regarding such things as work permits. The British labour supply would have been too narrow. But Paris and Brussels could do this too, were it not for other restraining factors. The first of these are onerous hiring and firing regulations that are poison in a fiercely competitive business where there has to be talent on board to prepare competitive tenders, but also the freedom to let staff go if the tenders don't win. As for EU labour market laws: all three companies are law-abiding employers, but the London company does not find itself constrained by EU laws. Nor do Paris and Brussels, since they are really constrained by French and Belgian laws that go way beyond what EU law requires.

The moral of this story is that freedom of employment in the EU labour market is vital for high-tech, creative service sectors on which London thrives, while national regulations in France and Belgium are problems for which the EU is not the culprit. But secession could mean immigration quotas and bureaucratic procedures for other Europeans to be hired in the UK.

The crude argument that 'Brussels red tape' is suffocating the economies of the UK and the whole of the EU into stagnation is hardy convincing therefore. Clumsy national regulatory policies in the countries ranked in the middle and lower categories above, coupled to systemic problems in the eurozone system, are more to blame for the ongoing stagnation of the eurozone.

One proposal by Prime Minister Cameron is that reforms should be embedded in a new treaty. There are serious problems with this, however. As explained by Lord Hannay, this position is mainly advocated by two groups at opposite ends of the political spectrum: on the one hand those who would like to drastically reduce or 'deconstruct' the EU's competences, versus those who would like to push on to a 'fully-fledged federal Europe'.[34] In between there is a large body of member states and political parties that do not see the need for another treaty, and are politically averse to the prospects of another hazardous ratification process.

A further cautionary comment is due on Prime Minister Cameron's hope for a 'reformed EU'. Any broad reform process embracing a wide range of policies, such as for the EU or a national government, are complex operations with mixes of short, medium and long-term measures. To use more precise and realistic language the objective can surely be for 'a significantly reforming EU'.

Renegotiation. The UK's first act of renegotiation took place shortly after its accession on 1 January 1973 under Edward Heath's Conservative government. In the general election of February 1974 the Labour Party promised a renegotiation of the terms of accession, to be followed by a referendum to confirm membership. Negotiations centred on the UK's net contributions to the budget, which were high because it benefited relatively little from the agricultural policy. A so-called 'corrective mechanism' was agreed, and the referendum was carried with a 67% Yes vote in June 1975. However, this mechanism proved to be ineffective, and subsequently Prime Minister Thatcher, in November 1979, sought better terms under her negotiating slogan "I want my money back". A much more effective abatement mechanism was agreed, and guaranteed by inscription in the treaties. The mechanism has subsequently been amended, with extension to other member states that argued that they also were making excessive contributions. The corrective mechanism is inscribed in a treaty-level act (Own Resource Decision), whose content is therefore guarded by the unanimity rule.

---

[34] Lord Hannay, *Europe Daily Watch*, 13 November 2014, available online.

More remarkable, in the area of Schengen, justice and home office affairs, it has secured not only a block opt-out, but also the right to opt back in where it wants to, as shown in the course of 2014 when it opted out of 133 such measures and then opted back in to 35 of them. On the other hand, the government certainly does not want to opt out of the single market and related sectoral policies, or from EU foreign policy where important decisions are taken by unanimity.

Overall, this leaves little scope for meaningful renegotiation. The flexibility that the UK requests in its relationship with the EU is thus already a reality on a grand scale. With its important opt-out from the eurozone, the UK has been described as "having the best of both worlds",[35] i.e. to be fully in the single market while retaining flexibility over the exchange rate and monetary policy, which helped the UK to emerge from recession ahead of the eurozone.

There remain two areas of high political controversy, namely the free movement of persons within the EU, where the Prime Minister has already set out his agenda for negotiation, and certain labour market rules, where some specific demands might be expected. It remains to be seen how these issues will be treated, bearing in mind that they are subject to serious divisions of opinion within the UK itself, quite apart from questions of negotiability within the EU.

Repatriation. Finally, as regards repatriation the prime purpose of the Balance of Competence Review was to screen for those existing competences of the EU that should better be returned to the member states. In terms of precise legal concepts this meant first of all looking at the 'competences' of the EU as they are defined in the Lisbon Treaty. At this level the evidence is clear. In not one of the 32 reviews is evidence presented by predominant or even majority views to suggest that any existing competence should be deleted from the treaty. On the contrary, the predominant finding is that the competences of the EU are 'about right', and that they have often found a sensible balance, notably

---

[35] George Soros, http://openeuropeblog.blogspot.be/2014/03/book-review-george-soros-tragedy-of.html, 13 March 2014.

in the sphere of the shared competences between EU and national levels.

This is before asking the question of whether a proposal to delete a competence from the treaty would be negotiable with all the other member states of the EU, given that this would require unanimity. On this point, there can be little doubt that unanimity would be elusive, since while enthusiasm for individual competences may vary between member states, all competences have support from numerous member states. For example, the Netherlands, which has adopted a position closest to that of the UK on a more rigorous application of the principle of subsidiarity, is explicit in not advocating repatriation of competences.

This broad finding that the competences of the EU are 'about right' is because the actual system is far more sophisticated in practice than much public debate would suggest over how it strikes the balance between EU and national powers. This is because most EU competences are 'shared' with, or simply 'supporting' national competences.

The continuing processes of negotiation over the exercise of these competences provides for adjustments in the effective share of responsibilities. This is worked out as individual EU directives or regulations are defined. The legal basis at the treaty level may be fixed in simple terms, such as just naming 'transport' as a shared competence. But the reality is one of continuous evolution in the effective sharing of competences.

At the second level of individual directives or regulations, the Reviews throw up instances where the case is made for their repeal, or more often their reform with less onerous implementation costs. Whether moves to repeal or lighten EU laws may be called 'repatriation' or 'reform' is maybe a matter of opinion and to a degree an open semantic question. But it is still an important point for political debate, since 'reform', although a highly elastic term, is in principle an acceptable idea for all, whereas 'repatriation' is not. For present purposes we consider 'repatriation' to be about the deletion of competences at the treaty level. For all other sub-treaty changes to existing EU laws, either by repeal, amendment or new legislation, we may bundle them into the 'reform' category.

> *The evidence at a glance – reform, renegotiation, repatriation*
>
> **Reform** – *abundant agenda across most policies. UK one of the most active drivers of reform*
>
> *'Cut red tape' now high on EU agenda, meets a UK demand; but multiple national regulations often more costly*
>
> **Renegotiation** – *not much scope, since UK supports broad single market, has opts-out of euro and Schengen, and flexible opt-out/opt-in agreement for justice and home affairs*
>
> **Repatriation** - *no evidence for repatriating EU competences as defined in Lisbon Treaty; precise sharing of most competences between EU and member states found to be broadly appropriate. Detailed application through individual directives and regulations can be adjusted.*

3.   Contemplating secession[36]

Secession is provided for in Article 50 of the Lisbon Treaty (TEU), which says that a member state "may decide to withdraw from the Union". It goes on to say that the Union shall negotiate an agreement with the seceding state to determine the terms of withdrawal and make arrangements for their future relationship (see Box 4). This sounds straightforward, and indeed much political debate in the UK talks of secession in simple terms. This is not realistic, however, since secession would be a highly complex and hazardous process. It would be more like a long and expensive divorce.

The consequences of secession have to be assessed from several angles – legal, economic and political.

---

[36] Since hypothetical modalities and implications of secession are not much discussed in the Reviews, this section relies on the assessments of the authors, with contributions by Adam Lazowski who publishes more detailed analyses in "Withdrawal from the European Union and Alternatives to Membership", *European Law Review*, Issue 5, 2012, Sweet & Maxwell, and *Withdrawal from the European Union – a Legal Appraisal*, Elgar Publishing, 2015 (forthcoming).

Box 4. Secession procedure in Article 50 of the Lisbon Treaty

1. Any Member State may decide to withdraw from the Union in accordance with its own constitutional requirements.

2. A Member State which decides to withdraw shall notify the European Council of its intention. In the light of guidelines provided by the European Council, the Union shall negotiate and conclude an agreement with that State, setting out the arrangements for its withdrawal taking into account of the framework for its future relationship with the Union. That agreement shall be negotiated in accordance with Article 218(3) of the Treaty on the Functioning of the European Union. It shall be concluded on behalf of the Union by the Council, acting by qualified majority, after obtaining the consent of the European Parliament.

3. The Treaties shall cease to apply to the State from the date of entry into force of the withdrawal agreement or, failing that, two years after notification referred to in paragraph 2, unless the European Council, in agreement with the member State concerned, unanimously decides to extend this period.

4. For the purposes of paragraph 2 and 3, the member of the European Council or of the Council representing the withdrawing Member State shall not participate in the discussions of the European Council or Council or in decisions concerning it.

A qualified majority shall be defined in accordance with Article 238(3) of the Treaty on the Functioning of the European Union.

5. If a State which has withdrawn from the Union asks to rejoin, its request shall be subject to the procedure referred to in Article 49.

Legal aspects. There is now a great mass of EU law that has entered the UK's statute books. The fundamental legal question is what would happen when, to quote Article 50.3, "the Treaties shall cease to apply..." This would depend on the terms of the withdrawal agreement. While one cannot forecast what this might consist of, there are quite a number of legal points on which some substantive comment is possible.

Secession would, from an internal point of view, first of all mean repealing the European Communities Act of 1972, which facilitates the direct application of EU law in the UK. The two main categories of EU laws, directives and regulations, have to be considered separately.

For EU directives, it is in their nature that they will have been 'transposed' into the national legislation of the UK. This means that their substantive content will continue to stand as UK law, and so in this case does not "cease to apply", unless the UK decided to change or repeal the UK laws in question. Many such directives concern technical norms for products or for regulating service sectors. While this so far sounds a comfortable proposition, the UK would have to decide where it wanted to be in relation to the mass of single market law. Under the EEA option discussed further below the UK would keep *all* single market law on its statute book. However, if it chose instead to be more selective in deciding which of its UK laws implementing EU directives it would continue with, it would face the loss of guaranteed access to the single market.

As for EU regulations, these are directly applied by EU law on actors in the member states, subject to enforcement by national courts and interpretation by the European Court of Justice. This body of law would clearly cease to apply, except to the extent that the UK had in any case enacted its own autonomous laws to supplement EU regulations. But to set out clearly and operationally what this would mean would be a major task of legal research, which has not been undertaken. For the single market there are many regulations and directives, so again the UK would have to choose whether to reinstate such regulations wholly or only selectively; in the latter case there would be the same risks for continued access to the single market.

Overall, this would be a huge task of combing through all the existing stock of EU directives and regulations in order to decide what to retain and what to discard. The provision that the treaties would cease to apply at the latest two years after the request to secede looks implausible. It could be agreed to extend this period, as allowed for under Article 50.3, but the downside of this would be a continued state of legal uncertainty facing business in Britain.

As regards the EU's many international agreements, these would cease to apply as between the UK and third countries. The EU has 794 bilateral agreements (treaties) in force, and 251 agreements with multilateral organisations. Since the UK would cease to be represented in all these agreements, it would have to decide whether to seek to clone the EU's agreements for itself bilaterally, or to negotiate its own different agreements. This would mean that the UK would have negotiate afresh all agreements that are relevant for it, which would certainly include all trade agreements. The UK would remain a member of the World Trade Organisation, but would have to negotiate afresh any terms of its membership that might differ from those of the EU. The task of negotiation or renegotiating the EU's bilateral trade agreements would be difficult because these have tended to become increasingly 'deep and comprehensive', which is reflected in the growing amount of complex regulatory matter that they include (for many service sectors such as finance, transport, business services, intellectual property rights, government procurement etc.). These agreements involve either, as in the case of the TTIP negotiations with the US, extremely complex and tough negotiations over regulatory convergence or mutual recognition or, as in the case of neighbouring states in east Europe and the Balkans, a lot of reliance on EU law as the common model. How the UK would work out its own deals alongside the agreements made or being negotiated by the EU is not easy to foresee. The third countries would regard the UK as a useful but second-level trading partner compared to the EU, and would cut no quick and favourable deals with the UK that might as a precedent prejudice their major interests in securing the best deal with the EU. This brings us into the economic implications of secession more broadly.

Economic aspects. A number of theoretical economic options can be described in relatively concrete terms, and these deserve to be spelt out in some detail since the stakes are so high.[37]

Simplistic big-bang exit. Some people who have very strong feelings about wanting secession, and who have not studied the workings of the British economy inside the EU, may be attracted by the idea of 'simply leaving'. This might be thought to mean an

---

[37] The scenarios in this section have been well analysed in "The Economic consequences of leaving the EU", final report of the CER Commission on the UK and the EU single market, Centre for European Reform, June 2014.

act of parliament renouncing the Act of Accession, and deleting from the statute book all legislation that has been required by EU membership. But it is inconceivable that any British government would do this, since it would put the British economy into a state of legal void on a grand scale: a 'mad' option. As mentioned above, there would have to be deep and no doubt long negotiations with the EU over the future relationship, and deliberations at home over what to do with the existing stock of EU legislation, and these are spelt out in more detail in the following scenarios.

European Economic Area (EEA) membership. The least disruptive course would be to request accession to the EEA, thus joining Norway, Iceland and Liechtenstein. If this were to happen the UK would first have to accede to EFTA and its agreements with third countries. The EEA scenario would then mean retaining on the statute book all existing internal market regulations, as well as all future developments of EU laws in this area. In exchange the UK would retain guaranteed access to the EU internal market as if a full member state. A possible advantage is that the UK would, as a non-EU EEA member, be entitled to negotiate its own foreign trade policies with the rest of the world, but whether the UK could secure better deals with trade partners than the EU, with its much greater bargaining power, must be open to doubt. The political disadvantage of this scenario is that the UK would have no say in the ongoing development of EU internal market policies and laws, yet would remain obliged to implement them. This is why Prime Minister Cameron said in his Bloomberg speech that he would rule out this option.

Customs union, like Turkey. This is also a technically feasible option. However, it would in one respect be even more constraining than joining the EEA, since it would require the UK to continue to implement the common external tariff of the EU and to follow it in whatever would be decided in future international trade negotiations, either at the multilateral level in the WTO, or in bilateral trade agreements such as may be made with the US or Japan. This would contradict the typical secessionist position that the EU should go ahead alone to make even more liberal trading arrangements with the rest of the world than the EU. So this too is extremely unlikely to be favoured by any secessionist British government.

The so-called Swiss option. Switzerland and the EU developed a complex set of bilateral agreements after the Swiss decided by referendum not to join the EEA. Yet the bilateral agreements have partly re-assembled the content of the EEA, albeit in a highly complex way and without an adequate institutional framework guaranteeing robust enforcement. The scheme has been seen as a more flexible version of the EEA, but in reality it has not worked so well. The EU objects to what it calls a 'cherry-picking' approach, and to avoid this insisted on a provision according to which termination of any single agreement falling under the so-called 'Bilateral I' package of several agreements would lead to the termination of the other agreements. These provisions are now in prospect since in 2013 Switzerland voted to re-introduce quotas for immigration from the EU. Even before this happened, the EU had signalled its dissatisfaction with these arrangements with Switzerland, and so it is unlikely that the EU would be willing to replicate it with a seceding UK.

Simple WTO option. Here the UK would, as a WTO member state, revert to trading relationships with the rest of the world on the basis of the 'most-favoured-nation' clause. In the simplest case this could mean retaining the EU's external tariff regime for the rest of the world; if the UK's external tariff schedule were to be different this would have to be negotiated. In withdrawing from the EU and its customs union, the UK would also be withdrawing from all the EU's existing preferential trade agreements, which in fact cover much of the world. But the advocates of secession are mostly advocating a more liberal free trade regime with the rest of the world than the EU practises today, which leads on to a final scenario.

Radical free trade option. Advocates of the UK setting itself free to enjoy radically freer trade with the whole world than the status quo in the EU sometimes cite the models of Singapore and Hong Kong, which long ago adopted a zero-tariff free trade policy unilaterally with the whole world, as did Georgia in 2006. The UK would presumably be able to make a free trade agreement with the EU, but the question then would be how deep and comprehensive such an agreement might be. This would return to the content of the EEA and customs union options. If the UK did not join either the EEA or the customs union its exports would be subject to strategic uncertainty over the level of guaranteed access to the EU market, and with obligations to introduce 'rules of origin' procedures to test whether British exports had been sufficiently 'made in the UK' to qualify for free trade. The 'rules of origin' procedures are heavy bureaucratic formalities, costly to business, in outright contradiction of the objective to cut the burden of 'EU red tape': i.e., this would be adding red tape from which the UK is currently free.

There is the question of whether a British government would really want to be much more liberal than the EU is today. The main case in point is China, since the EU already has made free trade agreements with Korea, Canada, and several Latin American countries; has preferential trade deals with most of Africa; and is negotiating with India, Japan, the US, Brazil (or Mercosur) and others. The only major economies with which the EU is not at present negotiating are Russia and China. As regards Russia, the EU would be willing to make a free trade agreement if Russia showed real interest in this, which it does not. As regards China, the UK already imports from it five-times more than it exports ($10 billion exports, $52 billion imports in 2013). Would free trade with China risk UK industry being overwhelmed and devastated by the competition? Or might the argument be that China would see the UK as an attractive manufacturing base for the European market? This is highly unlikely for a UK outside the EU (or the EEA). The metaphor of the UK becoming an 'off-shore aircraft carrier' for foreign powers to attack the EU market is already being bandied about, and France would take the lead in preventing this. The option of free trade with China, combined with secession from the EU, would risk the worst of both worlds – devastating competition at home and exclusion from guaranteed access to EU markets.

There is also the question of how interested other major players would be to make special free trade agreements with the UK. The US case is the most important one in this instance. The EU and the US are currently engaged in a very complex negotiation over the TTIP, which seeks to go deeply into regulatory matters for goods and services. Given the extreme difficulty that the US administration has in getting any free trade deals through

Congress, it is unlikely that it would want to invest in a special deal with the UK, which would have to go over all the issues currently under negotiation with the EU. The US would be concerned not to make particularly favourable concessions to the UK that could then be used as precedents in their bigger bargaining stakes with the EU.

This short review reveals several theoretical options for a seceding UK's trading relationships with the EU and the rest of the world. But they all seem to be problematic, compared to remaining an influential liberal presence in the EU.[38] In short, there is no good option for a seceding UK's trading relationships. This may sound unduly pessimistic to secessionists. But no better scenario has been laid out for serious consideration. The reason is that

---

[38] No attempt can be made here to quantify the macroeconomic consequences of different scenarios. The only pretension to do so was a much publicised report, "The Europe report: A Win-Win Situation", August 2014, commissioned by the Mayor of London, Boris Johnson (www.london.gov.uk/sites/default/files/europe_report_2014_08.pdf).

The Mayor's economist, Dr Lyons, presents four scenarios in his background report in www.london.gov.uk/sites/default/files/europe_report_appendices_2014_08.pdf, with appendices in www.london.gov.uk/priorities/business-economy/vision-and-strategy/the-europe-report

The four scenarios for the 20 years until 2035 were i) 'business as usual', with a UK growth rate of 1.9% (i.e. continued member ship of the EU without major reform; ii) the EU with the UK undertakes major supply-side economic reforms, with continued UK membership, resulting in a UK growth rate of 2.75%; iii) the EU and UK undertake the same reforms as in ii) but the UK secedes, and sees a slightly lower growth rate of 2.5%; and iv) a scenario in which the seceding UK becomes more protectionist, and sees a 1.4% growth rate. The report does not explain the basis for these estimates, with no indication of the supposed time-path, even for the first five years, for example. In the absence of basic professional information on the basis of these numbers, the paper would not have survived peer review. In particular, scenario iii) looks like a mere political assumption, with secession resulting in a still much improved growth rate, since this was used by the Mayor to support the view that the UK could have a good future either in or out of the EU, hence the 'win-win' in the title.

Britain's economic structure is deeply enmeshed in the European economic fabric of complex supply chains for goods and services, which depends upon seamless connections across national borders. These structures have developed as a function of both EU membership and geography, and are the foundations of the UK's relative prosperity. While the physical geography will not change, the effective economic geography would. The only sound economic option for the secessionists would be to join the EEA, but that is rejected on political grounds. Why quit the EU but stay in the single market without a say in its future evolution, and without a voice in European foreign policy, when the UK already has opt-outs from the major policies it does not want to join: the euro, Schengen, much of justice and home affairs, and so on?

Views of the business community. Business leaders also have no clarity as to which of the above scenarios might be chosen by a British government negotiating secession. However, they do have a clear view of the costs of strategic uncertainty about whether Britain would be in or out, and of the negative consequences of any arrangement other than continued full access to the EU's internal market. This is expressed in several opinion polls among business leaders as well as in the statements of individual business leaders.

Of members of the Confederation of British Industries (CBI), 71% felt in a poll conducted by *YouGov* and published in September 2013 that membership of the EU had a positive or very positive impact on their businesses, whereas 13% felt that there was a negative impact. Seventy-five percent felt that secession would have a negative impact on foreign direct investment, and 86% felt that there would be a negative impact on their access to EU markets. Seventy-two percent of businesses felt that the UK currently has influence over EU policies that affect them.[39]

A similar poll, undertaken by the Manufacturers' Organisation, found that 85% of its members favoured continued

---

[39] *CBI/YouGov* survey, September 2013.

membership of the EU, while a third of manufacturers said they would be less likely to invest in the UK.[40]

A poll conducted by *Ipso/Mori* for *TheCityUK* of members in London's financial sector, published in December 2013, showed a majority of 84% favouring continued membership of the EU, with only 5% advocating exit. Ninety-five percent said that access to the single European market was important to the UK's future competitiveness, with 90% believing that exit from the single market and the EU would damage the UK's competitiveness. Eighty-eight percent felt that EU membership economically benefits the UK as a whole.[41]

These various polls all record overwhelming majorities, mostly in the range of 75-95%, in favour of remaining in the EU and its single market, and express concern for the damaging impact of secession for both domestic and foreign investment. Individual business leaders of both British and foreign enterprises are making personal statements along the same lines, with a sample listed in Box 5.

Box 5. Statements by business leaders on the prospect of British secession from the EU

"I think Britain pulling out of the EU would be a blow to business, without question. From a business point of view it would be a mistake for the UK." *Willie Walsh, CEO of International Airlines Group, which includes British Airways.*

"Being a member of the EU bestows the UK with multiple benefits. It is a very attractive place for investors, and not just in the financial sphere. If it splits with the EU, it's not clear what benefits will remain. You cannot be sure what the relationship would look like." *Moritz Kraemer, Chief Sovereign Ratings Officer, Standard and Poors rating agency.*

---

[40] The Manfacturers' Organisation, "Manufacturing: Our Future in Europe – Stronger Leadership, A Stronger Economy", October 2013.

[41] *TheCityUK*, "UK and the EU – a mutually beneficial relationship", December 2013.

"You will see less manufacturing, less investment, and some US companies would look at the UK differently. Now they see it as a bridgehead to the rest of Europe." *Richard Cousins, CEO of Compass Group Plc.*

"The UK is part of the European Union; that is very important. From the foreign investor point of view I hope that the UK will remain an EU member". *Toshiyuki Shiga, CEO of Nissan.*

"I wouldn't say we are relaxed, we regard it as a very big tail-risk to our business. Our people want to be in London. We would hate to pull it apart. Every European firm [in financial markets] would be gone in very short order". *Michael Sherwood, Vice-Chairman, Goldman Sachs.*

"I do not believe the city's pre-eminent position will survive if we lose our role as Europe's financial capital. I don't believe we can maintain that position if we are not part of the single market". *Gerry Grimstone, Chairman of TheCityUK.*

"Europe is the bedrock of our international trade. We can trade with other countries of course. But with Europe such a big partner, it makes sense to continue that relationship while also trading elsewhere". *Sir Roger Carr, former President of the CBI).*

"If we [the UK] were not within the EU, Siemens would make it quite difficult for me to continue to invest in those factories". *Juergen Maier, Managing Director of Siemens UK.*

"Britain must not gamble on its future in Europe. The stakes are enormous. It is naïve to think we can pull up the drawbridge and carry on as usual. The debate has to move on to how we can make Europe work to support jobs, growth and higher living standards". *Terry Scuoler, CEO of EEF, The Manufacturers Organisation.*

The losses to the UK from secession would further extend to a number of policies beyond the single market. As the Reviews above showed, the sectors of higher education and scientific research would be hard hit. Today's Europe of young professionals are the 'Erasmus generation', in which it is has become the norm for university students to spend at least a year on exchange in a university outside his or her country of origin. This translates into a profound impact on the attitudes of young Europeans, for whom a return of former closeted national perspectives is an absurd proposition that no-one wants. Moreover, the British university system has been the single biggest beneficiary of Erasmus, for two reasons: the English language as a necessary professional skill, and the quality of the university system. The EU's research budget is now of substantial proportions compared to national research budgets, and has led to a very high degree of professional integration of Europe's research communities in both the natural and social sciences. The UK has again been a prime beneficiary of EU research funding, with its research institutions achieving outstanding success in winning competitive research contracts. Secession would mean putting all this at risk, or at best placing the UK in the position of supplicant to obtain the best cooperation agreement possible from the EU, from the position of a second-class associate.

Advocates of secession have to reflect on how tough would be the negotiations to obtain from the EU arrangements that would do the least damage to its interests in relation to the single market, and other programmes such as for education and research. There can be little doubt on the nature of the political context for such negotiations. The UK would be choosing a course of action that, while intended purely for the pursuit of its national interests, would mean inflicting grave reputational damage on the EU and the 'European project' as a whole. The EU would be little inclined to grant to the UK special favours in exchange.

Political implications. The foreign policy review contains assessments that the EU serves as a 'multiplier' of UK interests in the world, whereas outside the EU the UK would be regarded as a less significant actor in the world. Secession would therefore be a 'de-multiplier' of these interests. While these are matters of subjective judgement, there is no doubt about the position of the US, whose importance to the UK would surely increase in the event of secession from the EU. President Obama himself has politely but clearly stated that he values the UK as an influential member of a strong EU.[42] Today the EU is represented in the UN

---

[42] White House, Office of the Press Secretary, "The president underscored our close alliance with the United Kingdom and said that the United States values a strong UK in a strong European Union, which makes

Security Council by two permanent members, France and the UK. Both benefit from being broadly perceived by others to be representing Europe. For the UK this would be diminished by secession, and its position in the Security Council would be increasingly seen as an anachronism compared to the positions of Brazil, India, Germany and Japan, which have no such privilege. France, on the other hand, would be more clearly in a position 'to speak for Europe' there.

The argument that the UK needs to give greater attention in its foreign policy to the rising powers is hardly contested. But the question is whether this would be hindered or helped by secession. There is a clear tendency among EU member states to pay more attention to the rising powers, especially China. Germany has been in the lead in building up its bilateral strategic relationship with China. There is nothing to prevent the UK from pursuing these interests bilaterally from within the EU, but every reason to expect that UK leverage in such relations would be diminished if it had no voice in EU affairs.

The UK's reputation and relationship with the rest of the EU should also be assessed. A seceding EU would be seen as delivering a devastating blow to the European ideal. And what is the European ideal? It has two pillars. The first was recognised in the Nobel Peace Prize awarded in 2013 for the EU's historic, undisputed achievement in transforming the Europe of centuries of war into what political scientists call a "security community", which is an area of zero-threat perceptions between the member states. For those who take this for granted, even now while observing the centenary commemorations of the First World War, one has to look no further to the EU's immediate neighbourhood of Russia and Ukraine to appreciate what this means.

The second pillar concerns the values of democracy, human rights and the rule of law, to which the UK has made seminal contributions from the Magna Carta of 1215 through to the founding of the Council of Europe and its European Convention for Human Rights and Fundamental Freedoms and European

---

critical contributions to peace, prosperity, and security in Europe and around the world", 17 January 2013.

Court of Human Rights. British secessionists would like to withdraw from both the EU and obligations to respect rulings of the European Court of Human Rights. The rest of the EU would look on in dismay at this perceived undermining of fundamental European values, with approval coming only from the Kremlin, which would be quietly welcoming the disintegration of the EU.

Finally, there is the issue of how British secession would affect the internal politics of the UK, and in particular relations with Scotland, Wales and Northern Ireland. The political scenario for secession from the EU is that it would be led by the Conservative Party and its MPs from England, with support from the UKIP party. During the campaign leading to the Scottish referendum in September 2014, Scottish nationalists were clearly in favour of remaining in the EU. In the event of UK secession from the EU, it can be expected that Scottish nationalists would renew their demands for secession from the UK and at the same time seek to negotiate membership of the EU as an independent state. This is supported by opinion polls that show a larger degree of support for the EU in Scotland than in England.[43] Following the September 2014 referendum sensitivities between London and Edinburgh remain, notwithstanding the majority rejection of secession from the UK. The process of ensuring enhanced autonomy for Scotland remains a complex matter constitutionally and a highly charged one politically. In short, a referendum over the EU in 2017 or earlier is highly likely to aggravate the Scottish question.

There are also sensitivities in Wales and Northern Ireland, most practically around the role of the EU's Regional Development Fund. As the Review on cohesion reported above shows, there is opposition in Wales, Northern Ireland, and Scotland to the idea that the Fund be discontinued for the relatively rich EU member states, including the UK.

Overall, the secession scenario would not be good news for trust between England and the other three nations of the UK. How

---

[43] In the poll cited here, opinions in the UK as a whole were evenly divided over whether to remain in or quit the EU, whereas in Scotland there was a 2:1 majority for remaining in (http://survation.com/poll-for-sky-news-reveals-breadth-of-opinion-over-europe/).

damaging it would be is hard to say, but the risk of secession being poison to the politics of Northern Ireland and Scotland, each in their very different contexts, has surely to be taken seriously.

The evidence at a glance - secession

Legal aspects: *procedures for secession exist, providing for a necessary withdrawal agreement. Would be a highly complex process of deciding how far to repeal statutes implementing EU law*

Economic aspects: *a selective repeal of EU single market law would risk the loss of guaranteed access to EU market. Damaging impact on investment, in the views of overwhelming majority of business leaders*

Only risk-free economic scenario would be to join Norway in the EEA, but that would mean loss of sovereignty compared to status quo

Political aspects: *loss of say in future of Europe. 'De-multiplier' of UK foreign policy influence in global affairs. US warns against this*

A referendum is likely to aggravate tensions between England and Scotland

NB This topic of secession was not systematically treated in Reviews. The above conclusions are entirely those of the authors

---

Appendix A. Balance of Competences Review - Schedule of the British Government's Work

Each item involves publication of a report of around 40,000 words.
Summer 2013 (published July 2013)

1. Single market report (synopsis)
   https://www.gov.uk/government/consultations/call-for-
   evidence-on-the-governments-review-of-the-balance-of-
   competences-between-the-united-kingdom-and-the-european-
   union

2. Taxation
   https://www.gov.uk/government/consultations/taxation-
   report-review-of-the-balance-of-competences

3. Food safety and animal welfare
   https://www.gov.uk/government/consultations/call-for-
   evidence-animal-health-welfare-and-food-safety-review

4. Health
   https://www.gov.uk/government/consultations/review-of-
   the-balance-of-competences-health

5. Development cooperation and humanitarian aid
   https://www.gov.uk/government/consultations/developme
   nt-cooperation-and-humanitarian-aid-report-review-of-the-
   balance-of-competences

6. Foreign policy
   https://www.gov.uk/government/consultations/foreign-
   policy-report-review-of-the-balance-of-competences

Winter 2013 (published in February 2014)

7. Single market – free movement of goods
   https://www.gov.uk/government/consultations/single-
   market-free-movement-of-goods-report-review-of-the-balance-
   of-competences

8. Single market – free movement of persons (published in July)
   https://www.gov.uk/government/uploads/system/uploads
   /attachment_data/file/335088/SingleMarketFree_MovementP
   ersons.pdf

9. Asylum and non-EU migration
   https://www.gov.uk/government/consultations/asylum-
   and-non-eu-migration-review-of-the-balance-of-competences

10. Trade & investment
    https://www.gov.uk/government/consultations/review-of-
    uk-and-eu-balance-of-competences-call-for-evidence-on-trade-
    and-investment

11. Environment & climate
    https://www.gov.uk/government/consultations/eu-and-uk-
    action-on-environment-and-climate-change-review

12. Transport
    https://www.gov.uk/government/consultations/eu-balance-
    of-competences-review-transport-call-for-evidence

13. Research
    https://www.gov.uk/government/uploads/system/uploads
    /attachment_data/file/279331/bis_14_592_balance_of_compet
    ences_review_government_reponse_to_the_call_for_evidence.
    pdf

14. Tourism, culture & sport
    https://www.gov.uk/government/consultations/call-for-
    evidence-culture-tourism-and-sport

15. Civil justice
    https://www.gov.uk/government/consultations/balance-of-
    competences-review-call-for-evidence-on-civil-judicial-
    cooperation

Summer 2014 (published in July 2014)

16. Single market – free movement of services
https://www.gov.uk/government/consultations/review-of-uk-and-eu-balance-of-competences-call-for-evidence-on-the-single-market-free-movement-of-services

17. Single market – financial services and free movement of capital
https://www.gov.uk/government/consultations/balance-of-competences-review-single-market-financial-services-and-the-free-movement-of-capital

18. EU budget
https://www.gov.uk/government/consultations/balance-of-competences-review-eu-budget

19. Cohesion policy
https://www.gov.uk/government/consultations/review-of-uk-and-eu-balance-of-competences-call-for-evidence-on-cohesion-policy

20. Social and employment policy
https://www.gov.uk/government/consultations/review-of-uk-and-eu-balance-of-competences-call-for-evidence-on-social-and-employment-policy

21. Agriculture
https://www.gov.uk/government/consultations/agriculture-report-review-of-the-balance-of-competences

22. Fisheries
https://www.gov.uk/government/consultations/fisheries-review-of-the-balance-of-competences

23. Competition and consumer policy
https://www.gov.uk/government/consultations/review-of-uk-and-eu-balance-of-competences-call-for-evidence-on-competition-and-consumer-policy

24. Energy
https://www.gov.uk/government/consultations/energy-review-of-the-balance-of-competences%20

25. Fundamental rights
    https://www.gov.uk/government/consultations/balance-of-competences-fundamental-rights-review

Autumn 2014 (published December 2014)

26. Economic and monetary union
    https://www.gov.uk/government/consultations/economic-and-monetary-policy-review-of-the-balance-of-competences

27. Police and criminal justice
    https://www.gov.uk/government/consultations/police-and-criminal-justice-review-of-the-balance-of-competences

28. Information rights
    https://www.gov.uk/government/consultations/balance-of-competence-review-information-rights

29. Education, vocational training and youth
    https://www.gov.uk/government/consultations/education-vocational-training-and-youth-review-of-the-balance-of-competences

30. Enlargement
    https://www.gov.uk/government/consultations/eu-enlargement-review-of-the-balance-of-competences

31. Cross-cutting areas: voting, consular, statistics
    https://www.gov.uk/government/consultations/voting-consular-and-statistics-review-of-the-balance-of-competences

32. Subsidiarity & proportionality
    https://www.gov.uk/government/consultations/subsidiarity-and-proportionality-review-of-the-balance-of-competences

INDEX